Building a National Health-Care System

*A Statement on National Policy
by the Research and Policy Committee
of the Committee for Economic Development
April, 1973*

Single copy . . . $1.75

Printed in U.S.A.
First Printing April 1973
Design: Harry Carter
Library of Congress Catalog Card Number: 73-75244
International Standard Book Number: 0-87186-049-X

Committee for Economic Development
477 Madison Avenue, New York, N.Y. 10022

Contents

The Responsibility for
CED Statements on National Policy

This statement has been approved for publication as a statement of the Research and Policy Committee by the members of that Committee and its drafting subcommittee, subject to individual dissents or reservations noted herein. *The trustees who are responsible for this statement are listed on pages 5 and 6. Company associations are included for identification only; the companies do not share in the responsibility borne by the individuals.*

The Research and Policy Committee is directed by CED's bylaws to:

"Initiate studies into the principles of business policy and of public policy which will foster the full contribution by industry and commerce to the attainment and maintenance of high and secure standards of living for people in all walks of life through maximum employment and high productivity in the domestic economy."

The bylaws emphasize that:

"All research is to be thoroughly objective in character, and the approach in each instance is to be from the standpoint of the general welfare and not from that of any special political or economic group."

The Research and Policy Committee is composed of 60 Trustees from among the 200 businessmen and educators who comprise the Committee for Economic Development. It is aided by a Research Advisory Board of leading economists, a small permanent Research Staff, and by advisors chosen for their competence in the field being considered.

Each Statement on National Policy is preceded by discussions, meetings, and exchanges of memoranda, often stretching over many months. The research is undertaken by a subcommittee, with its advisors, and the full Research and Policy Committee participates in the drafting of findings and recommendations.

Except for the members of the Research and Policy Committee and the responsible subcommittee, the recommendations presented herein are not necessarily endorsed by other Trustees or by the advisors, contributors, staff members, or others associated with CED.

The Research and Policy Committee offers these Statements on National Policy as an aid to clearer understanding of the steps to be taken in achieving sustained growth of the American economy. The Committee is not attempting to pass on any pending specific legislative proposals; its purpose is to urge careful consideration of the objectives set forth in the statement and of the best means of accomplishing those objectives.

4.

6.

Dedicated to

Joseph C. Wilson
1909-1971

under whose guidance
the studies leading to this statement
were begun

Foreword

American medical science has made great advances in curing disease, easing human distress, and prolonging life. Yet unavailable to many people and even whole areas of the nation—the richest nation in the world—are the services required for adequate medical attention. Equally heartbreaking is the severe financial hardship that can and often does result from serious illness.

After nearly a decade of mounting debate, the nation is nearing the point of taking decisive action to remedy the inadequacies of its health-care system. The main question now remaining is which among the many suggested reforms offer the greatest likelihood of proving practical and effective—and at the same time affordable by the nation without a substantial inflationary effect.

Those chiefly adversely affected are the poor and otherwise disadvantaged. But many middle-income families also pay a heavy human price because health services are unavailable or overstrained, and because a long or expensive illness reduces them to poverty. And the nation generally pays a steep financial price as the cost of care escalates. Indeed, even as the nation debated the issue, its health-care bill increased sharply. Between 1965 and 1972, national health expenditures rose from $39 billion to $83 billion, or from 5.9 per cent to 7.6 per cent of GNP.

We believe that the goal of providing adequate care for all will continue to elude the nation even though vastly greater financial resources are poured into the system as presently constituted. At the same time, we believe we have given appropriate consideration to the national and the personal cost. To allow overspending on human needs for health care would simply create the human misery of inflation, with its agonies for the elderly and the poor.

This Committee proposes that the system be restructured through a series of actions to be taken in both the public and the private sectors, building on strengths and potentials where these exist. For example, extension of the present private health-insurance system to all employed persons would be an essential part of the system; so likewise would be the development of more effective regional agencies for comprehensive health-care planning.

Phasing is an indispensable element in this proposal. If widespread disappointment as well as further escalation of costs is to be avoided, it is crucially important in the development of a national health-care system to phase the financing of benefits offered to people—to keep the system in step with its actual capacity to deliver service and to pay its share of the cost.

The studies leading to this statement were begun under the chairmanship of the late Joseph C. Wilson, a CED trustee whose sudden and untimely death occurred in late 1971. Joseph Wilson made a special and important contribution to this cause. As chairman of the Governor's Steering Committee on Social Problems, established by Governor Nelson A. Rockefeller of New York, he guided the Steering Committee's influential 1970 study of health and hospital services and costs. Both CED and the Steering Committee greatly benefitted through the exchange of people and research in the health field, as they had earlier in their mutual studies of the public welfare system.

Joseph Wilson's great capacity for managing and organizing, which made him a distinguished industrialist, was notably strengthened by a compassionate understanding of human needs and aspirations. It was in this spirit that he approached public affairs, and it is our hope that we have faithfully reflected this spirit in carrying out his urgent and unfinished commitment. We also note with regret the passing of another subcommittee member, J. Douglas Colman, president of Associated Hospital Service of New York, who died in December 1972.

On behalf of the Research and Policy Committee, we thank The Robert Wood Johnson Foundation, The Commonwealth Fund, Herman Goldman Foundation, Inc., The Searle Foundation, and The D & D Foundation for their generous aid in funding our studies. We also extend appreciation to the many CED trustees, nontrustee members of the subcommittee, advisors, and staff members who gave valuable assistance in the preparation of this statement, and particularly to the Project Director, Jerome Pollack, and the Associate Project Director, Carl Rieser.

Philip M. Klutznick, *Chairman*
Marvin Bower, *Co-Chairman*
Research and Policy Committee

9.

Figure 1:
Gross Enrollment and Estimated Total Net Enrollment Under Private Insurance Plans, 1940-1970

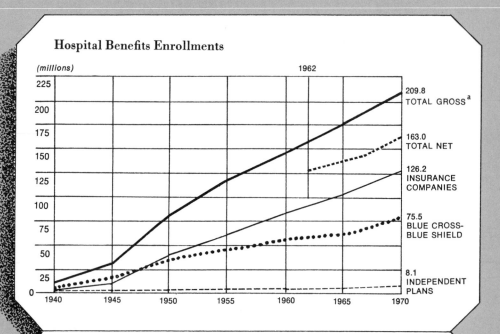

Hospital Benefits Enrollments

Surgical Benefits Enrollments

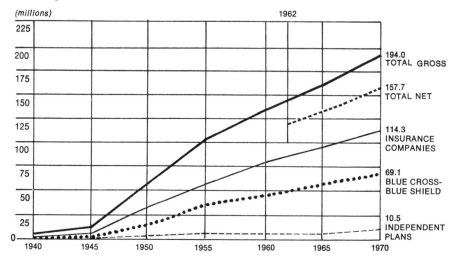

a/ Gross enrollment contains duplication because of multiple coverage of individuals through supplementary plans and policies. The net number of different persons covered (which eliminates duplication) is estimated for 1962 and 1967 by the Social Security Administration on the basis of household surveys. The 1970 estimate is derived by applying HIAA percentage increase in net enrollment to the 1969 estimate (not shown).

Source: U.S. Social Security Administration, *Social Security Bulletin*, Vol. 35, No. 2 (February 1972), p. 8.

Chapter One

Introduction
and Summary of
Recommendations

T his statement proposes a program
for improving the organization and financing of health services in the
United States to assure for all access to health care that is both adequate
and within the means of society and individuals. The world's wealthiest
and most economically advanced nation should not aspire to less than
this for its people. Furthermore, we believe that such a goal is within
grasp. Despite shortcomings that deny adequate health care to many
Americans or pose financial burdens for them, the health-care system
has strengths and resources that if properly nurtured and utilized can
eradicate these inequities. This can be achieved given vigorous pursuit
of the goal set forth above and the requisite time to relate access to health
care to needed improvements in the delivery system.*

Without question the United States possesses some of the finest
hospitals, physicians, and medical centers in the world. The magnitude of
our health-care enterprise is formidable. No less than 4.4 million people
are employed in the various health occupations, and there are some 3 million beds in hospitals and other inpatient facilities. Spectacular advances
have been made in the control of numerous diseases. In recent years there

*See Memorandum by MR. D. C. SEARLE, page 87.

have been notable decreases in mortality rates and corresponding extensions of the expectation of life, even though by these indices the nation now lags behind some other developed countries. Yet services have developed unevenly, resulting in a mixture of technical virtuosity and inadequacies in the delivery of minimum essential care.

For inner-city dwellers, the inadequacies frequently result from a decline in medical resources—decrepit buildings, overburdened staffs, and reduced service. But dissatisfaction with medical services is by no means confined to the poor. For people able to pay for care in small towns and rural areas, the problem may be the scarcity—even the lack—of medical services. The American Medical Association has identified 132 counties, with a combined population of nearly a half-million people, in which there is no civilian doctor. In many areas of the country, the problem is the unavailability of necessary specialists; for example, the ratio of specialists in the six least affluent states is half that of the ratio in the six most affluent.*

People generally — whether they are affluent, poor, urban, suburban, or rural—experience difficulties in securing adequate primary care. For over forty years the number of primary-care physicians has remained static (at about 120,000) while the population has soared, and until rather recently there has been little effort to redress this imbalance either through training programs or functional reorganization of services.*

The nation's health services have retained the organization — or lack of it — that may have been adequate for the health needs of an earlier era. As the major health problems shifted from acute to chronic diseases and toward conditions requiring more extended attention, the system failed to develop a continuous form of care to replace that based on episodic treatment. It also failed to shift from the concept of *sick* care to *well* care.

Health insurance has made dramatic advances in reducing for the majority of Americans the economic risks resulting from medical treatment. The great increase in coverage of the population by private insurance is illustrated in Figure 1, which traces enrollment in hospital and surgical plans over thirty years. The net number of persons covered by some form of private insurance, when duplication of coverage is eliminated, is now more than 160 million. This represents slightly more than 80 per cent of the population; at most about 50 per cent were covered only two decades ago.

---

*See Memoranda by MR. D. C. SEARLE, pages 88 and 89.

Figure 2: Personal Health-Care Expenditures by Source of Funds, Fiscal Years 1950 and 1972

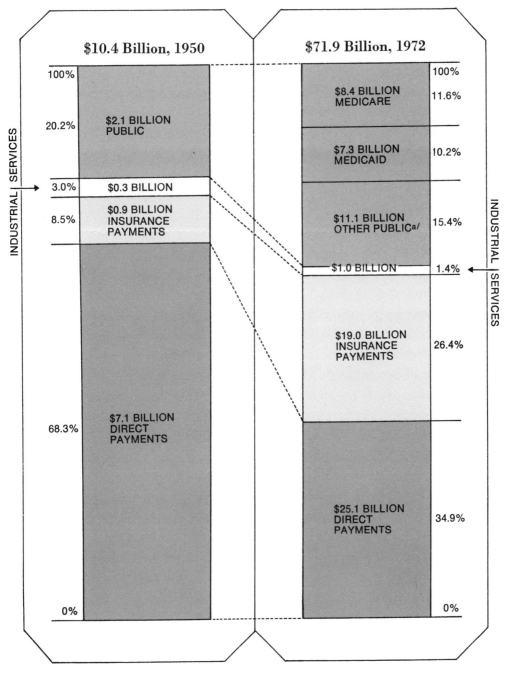

a/Includes workmen's compensation medical benefits, general hospital and medical care (primarily mental and charity hospitals), Defense Department hospital and medical care, veterans hospital and medical care, maternal and child health services, school health, O.E.O. neighborhood health centers, medical vocational rehabilitation, and temporary disability insurance.

Note: Some numbers do not total, due to rounding.

Sources: U. S. Social Security Administration, *Social Security Bulletin*, Vol. 35, No. 1 (January 1972), p. 13; newly released data for 1972 were obtained from U. S. Social Security Administration, Office of Research and Statistics.

The predominant means by which most Americans have acquired health insurance are the benefit plans of employers, which have a history dating back more than a century. Health insurance is part of a package of employee benefits commonly including pensions, sickness benefits, and group life insurance. By 1970, slightly more than 150 million persons—60 million employees and 90 million dependents—were covered by health insurance under these plans. The expenditures of employees and employers together on health-insurance premiums under these private plans in 1970 approached $14 billion.

The coverage of the private health-insurance system has been augmented by the government in recent years with the enactment of the Medicare program in 1965 to provide the elderly with hospital and medical insurance. This has brought coverage to 21 million Americans over sixty-five, and in addition some 1.7 million disabled persons are now being brought into the program. Under Medicaid, initiated in 1966, the federal and state governments share costs of medical care for the medically indigent, including welfare recipients.

Despite these great advances in coverage, gaps in health insurance persist. It has been variously estimated that 20 to 40 million people in the United States are without any health-insurance protection. The majority of these are poor and near-poor, nonwhite, unemployed — in general the disadvantaged. Medicaid was of course intended to finance health services for many of these people, but the program has failed to achieve its purpose, in part because of the welfare approach it has applied to health care. However, the flaws of the present financing system, while affecting most seriously the indigent, are not confined to this group. Millions of employed workers have no coverage.[1] Also, because of shortcomings in many existing plans, millions of other people who *are* covered have inadequate protection from the financial consequences of ill health.

The United States devotes a greater share of gross national product to health care than any other nation. The amount of money spent for this purpose should provide better care for all its people. While it is true that U.S. health services have broadened in scope, and are used with a greater frequency and intensiveness, costs have risen beyond the capabilities of many people and the local levels of government. Total national health expenditures climbed from $12 billion in 1950 to $83 billion in

---

1/"These are the employees of smaller concerns, especially in service trades, and casual workers . . . In case of serious illness, long periods of unemployment, early death of the wage earner, these families are apt to become dependent on relief." Marion B. Folsom, "Millions of Workers Still Lack Adequate Benefits," in Clarence C. Walton, ed., *Business and Social Progress* (New York: Praeger, 1970), p. 98.

Figure 3: Proportion of Consumer Health-Care Expenditures Met by Private Health Insurance, 1950-70

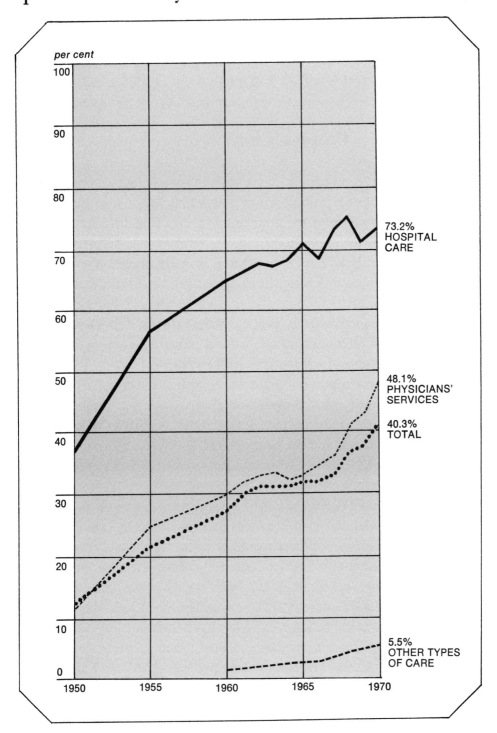

Source: U. S. Social Security Administration, *Social Security Bulletin*, Vol. 35, No. 2 (February 1972), p. 19.

1972, or from 4.6 per cent to 7.6 per cent of GNP. By far the largest element in the increase in expenditures for personal health care since 1950—nearly one-half—is attributed to price rises rather than to greater utilization of services and the introduction of new techniques. The rate of inflation in the cost of medical services since 1960 has averaged well over half again as much as that of consumer prices generally, and has even exceeded the rate of inflation in the cost of housing.

Proposals for Change

The country's awareness of the growing inadequacies of care has produced a number of proposals for national programs, a number of them stressing in particular the financing aspects of health care.

In 1967, Governor Nelson A. Rockefeller proposed legislation for health insurance in New York State with the evident intention of opening up national debate on this issue. Four years ago, the Committee of National Health Insurance (also known as the Committee of One Hundred), originated by the late Walter P. Reuther, began to develop a widely discussed proposal. With modifications, this has gained the support of organized labor in general as the Kennedy-Griffiths Health Security Plan. The Administration has proposed a National Health Insurance Partnership, and among the many other proposals before Congress are those sponsored by the insurance industry (Healthcare), the American Medical Association (Medicredit), and the American Hospital Association (Ameriplan). In mid-1971, there were pending no fewer than forty-five such bills for national health insurance.

There is wide divergence in the principles on which these proposals are grounded. Some would provide for comprehensive government-operated social insurance; others would offer tax credits or penalties to support and stimulate purchase of approved forms of health insurance; still others would provide for mandatory private insurance plus a program of benefits for the poor. There is little agreement on the crucial element of coverage—who should be covered?—or what benefits or services should be provided. Nor is there agreement on how much to spend for health protection; how much of this should be apportioned to the public and private sectors, and how much should be left to patients; or what methods of financing should be used. Wide differences exist as to the efficacy of competition, planning, and regulation, and in what ways the national program should seek to influence the provision of health services.

Central to these proposals is the pledge of access to health care as a right to all. Shortly after enacting Medicare, Congress reaffirmed its conviction that "fulfillment of our national purpose depends on promoting and assuring the highest level of health attainable for every person." There can be no question that one of the national goals should be adequate health care for all Americans.* The central question is how to convert the right of access for all into actual access for all—how to convert an aspiration into skills, services, facilities, and systems available to the people.

We believe that some kind of national health-care program, extending health-insurance coverage to all, will indeed be enacted in the near future. A coordinated approach to this is essential in order to avoid the danger of inflated health costs that do not produce increased services or increased availability and access to improved services.

In the past, the national mode of response has been to deal separately with each shortcoming of the system in a succession of crises—in facilities, manpower, financing, or social policy. We believe that this is no longer tenable and that a serious effort to improve health care must embrace (1) the restructuring and redeployment of the health-care delivery system, (2) an enlarged insurance system so designed as to reinforce the changes required in the delivery system, and (3) an effective planning and control structure. In this statement we outline the steps we believe should be taken to effect the transition to a universal health-care system.

Three Conclusions About the Present System

The program presented here is based on three conclusions derived from our study of the present system.

First, faulty allocation of resources is a major cause of inadequacies and inequalities in U.S. health services that result today in poor or substandard care for large segments of the population.**

While manpower, facilities, and services are lacking in some areas, as observed earlier, they are in excess in others. There is also functional as well as geographical maldistribution, causing most notably the nearly nationwide inadequacy in primary care while medical specialties often exceed requirements. The market mechanism works imperfectly in meet-

---

*See Memorandum by MR. OSCAR A. LUNDIN, page 89.
**See Memorandum by MR. D. C. SEARLE, page 89.

ing needs for health care; there is a distortion in incentives and pricing, and functions are poorly organized and often inefficient.* Nor has there been an adequate effort at overall planning. What confronts the United States is an essential industry—the nation's third largest in the numbers of people employed—that delivers vitally important services at a level far below its potential capability.**

Second, the task of assuring all people the ability to cope financially with the costs of health care has been made realizable by the substantial base of coverage now provided by both private and public insurance plans.

The dramatic alteration in the patterns of financing health care over the past quarter of a century or more is illustrated in several ways. Between 1950 and 1972, direct payments by individuals as a share of personal health expenditures were reduced from 68 per cent to 35 per cent of the total, as private insurance and public expenditures increased. However, as can be seen in Figure 2, direct payments have increased substantially despite the greater coverage, rising from approximately $7 billion to $25 billion. Other statistics show that about 50 per cent of the cost of hospital care is now paid for by some unit of government and private insurance pays for another 35 per cent; government pays for 25 per cent of the cost of physicians' services, private insurance for 35 per cent. For those people covered by private-health insurance, the carriers pay for about 70 per cent of consumer outlays for hospital care and nearly 50 per cent of outlays for physicians' services, as shown in Figure 3.[2]

There now exist large-scale, functioning mechanisms for the financing of health care in the United States. These can provide a firm base for further—and much needed—improvement and extension of the system so that it covers the entire population.

Third, unless step-by-step alterations are made in the means of delivering services and paying providers, closing the gaps in financing would overburden an inadequate system and offer little prospect of materially improving the quality and quantity of medical services or the health of the American people.

The very programs intended to help people meet rising costs have contributed unintentionally to further increases in cost.** For example, the most prevalent kind of health-insurance coverage is hospital care, whereas ambulatory-care benefits still are scantily insured; this has con-

2/These figures do not include the contributions by individuals and families to the cost of the premiums for health-care insurance.
*See Memorandum by MR. WAYNE E. THOMPSON, page 90.
**See Memoranda by MR. D. C. SEARLE, pages 89 and 90.

18.

tributed to the overuse of expensive hospital facilities at the same time that it has discouraged the development of badly needed ambulatory-care services. Likewise, reimbursing providers of care by tolerating the pass-through of costs has reduced or eliminated incentives for economy.

To pour large amounts of money into the present system through the expanded benefits of a national health-insurance plan would undoubtedly create further distortions in demand, pricing, incentives, and resource allocation without markedly improving services. We cannot stress too much the importance of scheduling benefits only when they can be delivered in care. We caution that whatever national health-insurance program is finally enacted will have to contain some provision for phasing to an adequate level of benefits by steps—not all at once.

Scheduling, Continuity, and Cost

Two basic alternative methods of phasing are possible in initiating a national health-care system. First, the insurance program can be deferred while the delivery system is being restructured in order that health services not be overwhelmed and false expectations raised. Or, second, the two programs can be introduced simultaneously, with the development of the financing system phased to the improvements in the delivery system. This, of course, assumes that proper design of the benefits as well as effective planning and supervision of the program will encourage development of new and more efficient systems of delivery. This second choice has the double advantage of bringing people into the system earlier and also of financing the development of improved health services largely through users' payments to providers.

There are two choices about benefits. A single high standard of benefits can be established at the outset, and phasing can take the form of bringing segments of the population successively under this protection (according to priorities based on need) until the population is covered universally. Or it is possible to start with a basic level of benefits covering all people immediately; those not already covered by insurance would receive these benefits, which would also serve as a floor under existing plans. The benefits would then be improved and broadened until eventually all people had the protection of a single high level of comprehensive benefits*—and the assurance that in fact these could indeed be realized in

---

*See Memorandum by MR. DANIEL F. EVANS, page 91.

terms of the delivery of services. Even taking into account the structural and administrative complexities inherent in choice number two, we believe that on balance it is preferable because it affects a larger number of people—the whole population in fact—at an earlier date.

The design of an interim system such as we propose puts heavy emphasis and reliance on continuity—on making fullest use wherever possible of those dynamic elements in the present system that have potential for evolution and development. Since the great majority of the nation's employees are now covered by health insurance, we see the incorporation of the massive, existing employer-based system into a national program as the most feasible way to move fairly quickly toward coverage of the entire population. Our program would require all employers to provide health-insurance coverage for all qualified employees and their dependents. Medicare would be continued for the aged and disabled. A third category would be established for all those not covered under these programs, through insurance financed on an income-related basis, with sharing of costs where appropriate by the federal government.

Very briefly, other features of our proposal include programs to foster new delivery systems. In particular, we want to encourage the development of prepaid comprehensive care for subscribing clientele or populations through health-maintenance organizations as the most likely means of improving efficiency in the management of health services. Finally, our plan provides a control and planning mechanism for the system at both the national and regional level in order to provide effective development of health benefits, facilities, functions, services, manpower, and systems.

Any changes recommended here and their prospective costs have to be viewed against alternatives. One alternative is the continuance of current practices with little change except for piecemeal add-ons; a second alternative is large-scale abrupt public assumption of present private functions. Past experience forces us to conclude that either course would only escalate inflationary tendencies and increase the cost per service.

The recommendations made here are intended to be inaugurated only as the system can absorb additional burdens. The synchronization of needed additional benefits with improvements in the system may increase costs at the outset to a degree, but in a reasonable period of time it should produce more coverage and better health care at less cost per unit of service. Timing is essential, or else money will again be poured into a system unable to handle the load with another round of inflation inevitable.

It is always difficult to estimate precisely the extra costs of a new set of recommendations dependent on the timing of achieved improvements in the health-care delivery system. The Department of Health, Education, and Welfare bases its estimates of the cost of various health-insurance proposals on four main factors: (1) a profile of present expenditures; (2) an estimate of transferred costs as that portion arising from the transfer of expenditures from one sector to another; (3) induced costs as the extent to which proposals might add to the nation's health expenditures by affecting the supply and demand of health care; and (4) tax adjustments as the increase or loss of revenue to the federal government. We have followed this methodology in estimating the cost of our proposal (see Appendix C).

Ignoring the timing aspects of these proposals, which will tend to slow up implementation until the system can absorb them, the maximum additional expense would be $5 billion in the first year as against anticipated expenditures if there are no changes in the system.* But since implementation of our recommendations would not become fully operative in one year, it is more likely that the gross initial addition to costs will be less than $5 billion. For the longer run, the direct additions to costs implied by the program should be offset at least in part by the better utilization of resources and cost reductions resulting from basic management improvements. Indeed, full implementation of our proposals might well lead to a lesser increase in total expenditures than is implied by present trends.**

Summary of Recommendations

The following are the major recommendations made by the Research and Policy Committee to bring about the restructuring and delivery of health care, the phasing and financing of a national health-care system, and the effective planning and use of resources. These are interspersed wth summaries of the supporting recommendations. The structuring of a national health-insurance program is described in Chapter 5.

---

*See Memorandum by MR. D. C. SEARLE, page 91.
**See Memorandum by MR. OSCAR A. LUNDIN, page 91.

We recommend enactment of a health-insurance program that would require a basic level of protection to be made available to all Americans regardless of their means, age, or other conditions. This coverage should be continuous, without interruptions during a hiatus in employment or for any other cause; treatment should not be delayed for determinations of liability for payment, and care should not be foregone or deferred because of inability to pay. First priority should be assigned to making insurance available to all for all of the benefits that can be provided promptly within the resources available on inauguration of the program. We recommend that those benefits be expanded in a phased progression geared to the availability of services, to the reorganization of the health system, to minimizing price inflation, and to achieving greater uniformity and effectiveness of coverage.*

Restructuring the Delivery of Care

Health services must be reorganized and new delivery systems must be developed so that the resources can be used to the level of their capabilities in bringing care to people. These measures are described in Chapters 3 and 4.

Basic to the establishment of a national health-care system is a determined and adequately supported program to make health services more accessible to people, all of whom will be entitled to receive basic benefits. Specifically, this will require a greatly accelerated development of ambulatory- and primary-care centers, particularly in areas of special need; mental-health centers; and especially organizations that assume responsibility for providing comprehensive and continuous care. We recommend that federal grants and loan guarantees be extended to encourage private and public construction of such agencies and activities, as certified by the appropriate health-planning agencies and authorized by the Secretary of Health, Education, and Welfare. Also of vital importance is the continuous financing of such services, through a national system that we propose, and the integration of components into a comprehensive program of health care in each region.

The close linking of the delivery and financing functions is essential to the effective organization of health services.

To achieve a national health-care system that stresses prevention as well as cure, we recommend (1) that financing be based on prepay-

*See Memorandum by MISS CATHERINE B. CLEARY, page 91.

22.

ment for an essential set of benefits, and (2) that to the maximum feasible extent providers of care be paid in accordance with fees and charges fixed in advance by agreement with providers and related to a budget that reflects efficient organization and procedure. We believe that the application of the concept of the health-maintenance organization represents an admirable and efficient response to such a payment system.*

Other recommendations concerning health-maintenance organizations call for diverse sponsorship by both profit and nonprofit groups able to qualify. Inducements and incentives should encourage participation in health-maintenance organizations by subscribers and staff, but participation by all should be entirely voluntary. HMOs should develop broad benefits and serve a cross section, both socioeconomic and racial, of people in their areas wishing to join.** Impediments to the formation of new comprehensive delivery systems by archaic legislation and rulings must be eliminated.

Phasing and Financing a National System

To achieve the transition to a universal system most readily and smoothly, the present health-care financing structures—employer-based plans and Medicare—would be retained, and a third category would be created to cover all other people, absorbing most of Medicaid.

We recommend that national health-insurance coverage be provided through a three-category system:

1. Employers should be required by statute to provide a minimum level of employment-based insurance protection for all employed persons and their dependents for specified basic benefits under qualified plans.

2. Medicare would continue to cover aged persons under the social-security system and those eligible for disability benefits under both the social-security and railroad-retirement acts, with certain modifications in benefit provisions.

3. Federally-sponsored community trusteeships should be established to assure basic benefits for all persons ineligible under the above categories. These would include the poor and near-poor,

---

*See Memoranda by MR. D. C. SEARLE, page 90, and by MR. ROBERT T. FOOTE, page 91.
**See Memorandum by MR. MARVIN BOWER, page 92.

people between jobs as well as the long-term unemployed, part-time employees not qualified for employment-based plans, and the self-employed. Also covered in this category would be aliens,* the temporarily disabled, and people regarded as uninsurable by customary insurance standards to the extent practically and legally feasible. Agencies of state and local government should be able to perform the trustee role if they are qualified.

A basic benefit standard would be applied to the employer-based and community-trusteeship plans, and this would be phased to provide increasingly better coverage. However, in view of the diversity of present plans, it will be necessary to allow latitude in applying new benefit standards.

We recommend that any employer already providing benefits that in the aggregate are equivalent to or in excess of the standards, though differing in some respects from them, should be held in conformance with the required plan. Administrative procedures and criteria should be developed to determine compliance. However, after a prescribed period, all plans would be required to comply with each benefit standard in addition to overall compliance.

In the case of small establishments particularly, there is a danger that contributions by many employers and employees to finance health insurance may exceed a manageable level.

We recommend that the premiums for employment-based plans be financed typically by employer and employee contributions. No employer or employee should be required to contribute more than a stipulated maximum proportion of the basic insurance premiums. However, there should be an exception to this principle in those cases where an employer has elected to bear more than his required share of the cost.** In order to limit the respective contributions both of employers and employees to the specified levels, an insurance pooling mechanism should be established.

Direct payments for care should be fixed, known, and predictable amounts that in total should not exceed a stipulated percentage of cost of treatment nor in the aggregate of family income.

The Medicare program in the second category would continue to be financed as at present, and a new financing arrangement would be developed for the third category.

---

*See Memorandum by MR. MARVIN BOWER, page 92.
**See Memorandum by MR. JOHN D. HARPER, page 92.

The insurance coverage under community trusteeships would be financed by general-revenue support for the poor and near-poor and, where appropriate, through a sliding scale of contributions according to such variables as income and family size. Persons whose income is below national poverty standards, whether or not they are receiving welfare assistance, should be relieved of both premiums and copayments; these should be financed by the federal government.

Another recommendation urges that the administration of Medicare should be given the added responsibility of overseeing the community trusteeships. More importantly, a new federal structure should be established to guide national policy regarding health insurance.

In order to assure an overall health-insurance policy and to achieve coordination among the component programs, we recommend the creation of a National Health Insurance Advisory Board, appointed by the President and serving in an advisory role to the Secretary of Health, Education, and Welfare. Its membership would comprise public members, as well as health practitioners, administrators, or educators.* The board would be responsible for reviewing the overall regulations directing the insurance program; the timeliness and appropriateness of scheduled phasing of benefits; and the guidelines for evaluating existing employment-based benefit programs and proposed changes in them for compliance. The board's report on the status of the program to the Secretary would be made available to Congress and the nation.

Structural changes within the health-care industry, particularly through the greatly increased emphasis on comprehensive care, should eventually help to stabilize costs. But until this occurs, direct wage-price controls may be needed.

Because market forces work imperfectly to supply health care at reasonable costs, we believe that it would be advisable during the inauguration of a national health-insurance program to keep governmental controls over some or all health-care fees, charges, and wages to avoid runaway costs during the transitional period.

Planning Use and Resources

An effective planning-administrative structure at the regional level is needed to bring together both the financing and delivery functions of health care. As described in Chapter 6, this agency would bring to

---

*See Memorandum by MR. DANIEL F. EVANS, page 92.

bear the new financial resources developed through the national health-insurance program to plan and foster improvements in the delivery system.

We recommend that wherever they exist the presently authorized comprehensive health-planning organizations ("B" agencies) be converted by order of the Secretary of Health, Education, and Welfare into Regional Health Service Agencies, that such agencies be established for all health service regions which lack them, and that their governing boards be appointed initially by the Secretary.* Their powers should be augmented to include the planning of facilities and resources, the review of those presently existing, and development of priorities for improvement. They should have authority to delegate tasks to other planning agencies handling these functions and to assume planning functions of other agencies that are performing inadequately. They should be empowered to encourage, support, and authorize organizations to develop comprehensive health-maintenance programs according to approved guidelines and standards for better service and lower cost. They should be responsible for supervising the quality of service and might be delegated as needed to administer price controls over health services in their areas. They also might organize and manage regional information and health-education networks and administer the Public Health Service programs in their areas.

Essential to the development of effective and efficient new health-delivery systems is the proper training and use of manpower—particularly of physicians' assistants and other allied manpower. Planning of manpower development should be coordinated on a national level.

We recommend increased support and development of health-manpower training programs following systematic central planning by a national health-manpower program located in the office of the Secretary of Health, Education, and Welfare. This office should have a central clearing function to coordinate the goals, data collection methods, and overall design of individual efforts into a broader base for support and evaluation. It should collaborate with the Department of Labor and other departments and agencies to integrate the efforts of the many separate programs of government.

An additional recommendation urges that licensure and certification requirements at the state level should be revised to increase job mobility and utilization of professional personnel.

---

*See Memorandum by MR. ROBERT T. FOOTE, page 93.

26.

Finally, to develop the appropriate planning, organization, and training needed to improve the nation's health-delivery system will require greatly intensified and sustained research and development.

We recommend that increasing public and private funds be made available for experimental and demonstration programs designed to improve the delivery of health care in amounts consistent with tooling up and with the capability of their prudent use. The responsibility for generating principles and standards for the expenditure of these funds should be vested with the Secretary of Health, Education, and Welfare in such a manner as to maximize their availability to agencies, both private and public, that are dedicated to and actively involved in the delivery of health care.

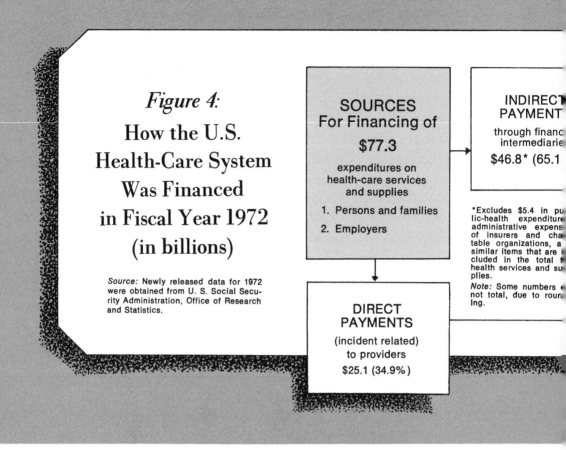

Figure 4:

How the U.S.
Health-Care System
Was Financed
in Fiscal Year 1972
(in billions)

Source: Newly released data for 1972 were obtained from U. S. Social Security Administration, Office of Research and Statistics.

SOURCES
For Financing of
$77.3
expenditures on
health-care services
and supplies
1. Persons and families
2. Employers

INDIRECT PAYMENT
through financ
intermediarie
$46.8* (65.1

*Excludes $5.4 in pu
lic-health expenditur
administrative expens
of insurers and cha
table organizations, a
similar items that are
cluded in the total
health services and su
plies.
Note: Some numbers
not total, due to roun
ing.

DIRECT PAYMENTS
(incident related)
to providers
$25.1 (34.9%)

Chapter Two

The Present
Health-Care System

Health-care services in the United States are operating under severe pressure. They have had to cope with complex problems in assimilating and applying unprecedented scientific and technological advances. Likewise, in responding to the changing needs of a growing and aging population, they have expanded exponentially in manpower, facilities, and other resources. But with growth and

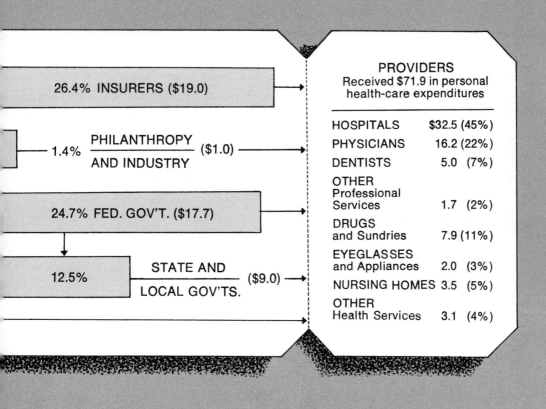

PROVIDERS Received $71.9 in personal health-care expenditures		
HOSPITALS	$32.5	(45%)
PHYSICIANS	16.2	(22%)
DENTISTS	5.0	(7%)
OTHER Professional Services	1.7	(2%)
DRUGS and Sundries	7.9	(11%)
EYEGLASSES and Appliances	2.0	(3%)
NURSING HOMES	3.5	(5%)
OTHER Health Services	3.1	(4%)

26.4% INSURERS ($19.0)

1.4% PHILANTHROPY AND INDUSTRY ($1.0)

24.7% FED. GOV'T. ($17.7)

12.5% STATE AND LOCAL GOV'TS. ($9.0)

change poorly related to priority of needs, the system is overwhelmed by the increasing burdens of care, just as those who pay for it are burdened by increasing cost.

There have been enormous increases in health expenditures over the past two decades (see Figure 5, page 41). Here, briefly, is what has occurred:

■ In 1950 national health expenditures totaled $12 billion, 4.6 per cent of gross national product, or $78 per capita.

■ In 1965 (on the eve of Medicare and Medicaid) health expenditures, already a matter of much concern, approached $39 billion, 5.9 per cent of GNP, or $198 per capita.

■ In 1972 expenditures were $83 billion, 7.6 per cent of GNP, or $394 per capita.

The present organization of services derives from an earlier era when the health enterprise was smaller and simpler. The concept of a system in which various components might be brought together into an organized, orderly arrangement was scarcely understood when the present system evolved. For many years the overriding need was for more physicians, more hospitals, more resources of other kinds. And even though the health services outgrew their form of organization several decades ago, the system continued to grow largely by accretion, without a necessary restructuring.

This piecemeal approach to the problems of health care has led to a serious maldistribution in manpower and facilities in terms of need. Four particularly significant distortions in the system now confront the nation.

Profile of the Health-Care System: Use, Demand, Resources

■ About two episodes of acute illness a year afflict the average American, causing him to seek medical attention or restrict activity for one or more days. In addition, roughly one-half of the American people report one or more chronic conditions such as heart disease, arthritis, mental and nervous conditions, or numerous other long-term impairments. These are currently the most common causes of medical care, disability, and death. In all, nearly three-fourths of the population visit or are visited by doctors in a year. The chronically ill pay for over 70 per cent of the visits to physicians.

■ The demands for service by the nation's 200 million people are enormous. Examinations by physicians are approaching 1 billion annually, averaging 4.6 visits per person in 1970. Some 32 million patients a year are admitted to hospitals as bed patients, and more than 181 million get hospital care as outpatients. Nearly 900,000 people reside in nursing and related homes. At least 1 billion drug prescriptions are filled annually while vast numbers of drugs are purchased over the counter.

■ The number of physicians is estimated at 345,000. Of the 312,600 nonfederal physicians, 264,000 are engaged in patient care—195,100 are in office practice, and 68,900 in hospital-based practice. Some 25,700 physicians are engaged in other professional activities such as medical teaching (5,200), administration (9,300), research (9,100), and other activities (2,100). The 29,200 federal physicians are largely involved in hospital-based practice

1. *Shortage of primary care.* Primary care has been defined as the kind of medical services that most people use most frequently for almost all of their health problems, and it likewise accounts for most services provided by doctors. Primary care helps open the door for people seeking hospital examinations and care. On it depends continuity of service for individual medical problems from preventive health maintenance, through evaluation of general discomfort and early complaints and symptoms, to care for chronic types of illness.

Physicians who fulfill this central function are in short supply, mainly because of the competition from such specialties as surgery that

(20,700), while almost all the rest of these physicians are involved in office practice, administration, and research. The remainder (3,200) are either inactive or unclassified, or their addresses are unknown.

■ Total manpower in the health field, approximately 4½ million, includes professionals and associated personnel engaged in clerical, maintenance, and similar work. This group constitutes some 5 per cent of the nation's total labor force, making health care the nation's third largest "industry" in terms of manpower. Using rounded numbers, there are 100,000 dentists; 140,000 pharmacists and aides; 35,000 optometrists, opticians, and assistants; 725,000 registered nurses; 400,000 practical nurses; and some 850,000 nursing aides, orderlies, and attendants. About 240,000 other personnel are engaged as engineers, scientists, sanitarians, technicians, and aides.

■ An enormous range and number of facilities play the important dual role of partly housing and partly organizing health activities. There are some 31,000 inpatient facilities (including nursing homes) in the United States with a total of nearly 3 million beds. They include 7,800 hospitals, 19,000 nursing and related homes, and a variety of 4,000 other types of inpatient housing. Other facilities include outpatient departments of hospitals, laboratories, group-practice clinics, mental health centers, public health agencies, opticianry establishments, rehabilitation centers, and the like. These are nearly as numerous as those that admit and board patients. The full range of health facilities also includes some 140,000 physicians' offices, nearly 85,000 dentists' offices, some 52,000 drug stores, numerous industrial health facilities, as well as patients' homes, which are often overlooked but are one of the most heavily used sites of care.

offer greater rewards in terms of prestige, self-esteem, and money.* This situation is far more damaging to the delivery of care than shortages in any single medical specialty. While the total number of physicians has increased somewhat in relation to the population, the ratio of those providing primary care (general practitioners, pediatricians, internists, obstetricians, and gynecologists) continues to decrease, dropping from 65 per 100,000 population in 1966 to 59 per 100,000 in 1970. Even if health-care delivery were nationally as efficient as the most productive medical organizations, there would still be a shortage of primary physicians.

The imbalance between the number of primary physicians and specialists has various complicating effects. For example, the number of patients seen per day varies by different types of physicians; specialists on the average see about one-fourth fewer people than do general practitoners.* Moreover, there is some evidence that an excess of some specialists—for example, surgeons—may lead to an excess of some treatments —for example, surgery.

2. *Uneven distribution of services*. The distribution of medical services in various sections of the country is closely linked to their affluence and appeal to physicians. This is illustrated by comparing recent data regarding physicians for six states with high per capita and household incomes (California, Connecticut, Illinois, New Jersey, New York, and Massachusetts) with data for an equal number of states with low incomes (Alabama, Arkansas, Louisiana, Mississippi, Tennessee, and South Carolina).**

The more-affluent states average 160 practicing physicians per 100,000 people, or almost double the 87 physicians per 100,000 people in the less-affluent states.[1] The gap in general practitioners is narrow—27 to 22 physicians per 100,000 people. But the differences in the availability of specialists is striking. The number of medical specialists per 100,000 people in the more-affluent states is 29 compared with 14 in the less-affluent; 35 compared with 23 surgical specialists; and 23 compared with 10 other specialists. There is a still greater difference in the number of physicians per 100,000 population in hospital-based practice: 46 compared with 18.

1/American Medical Association, *Distribution of Physicians in the United States, 1970* (Chicago: 1971). The figures above do not include doctors employed by the federal government.

*See Memoranda by MR. D. C. SEARLE, page 93.
**See Memorandum by MR. D. C. SEARLE, page 88.

Thus, there are significantly different modes of practice among the states. Within most states there are also enormous differences, with relatively fewer doctors in both rural and inner-city areas. Similar disparities are to be found among other categories of medical manpower.

3. *Surplus facilities.* In recent years the number of general hospital beds in the nation has increased at a greater rate than the population. Between 1963 and 1970 the ratio of beds per 1,000 people went up from 4.3 to 5.0—a significant rise of more than 16 per cent in the face of increasing doubt regarding the justification for hospital expansion.

Most studies show that some patients in the hospital either do not need to be there or stay too long. Hospitalization is used far less in better organized systems, where the incentives work to treat patients on an ambulatory basis when this is appropriate rather than as inpatients. Furthermore, hospitals taper off their activities during weekends, and thus put patients "in storage" over weekends in hospital beds at great expense and sometimes to the detriment of their care. Fewer beds would be needed if the hospital operated more fully throughout the entire week. In many areas there is unnecessary duplication of centralized hospital care and at the same time a critical shortage of ambulatory centers, facilities for "halfway" care, organized home care, and numerous other urgently needed programs.

Although hospitals had already been built to excess by the 1960s, much the same situation has been repeated in nursing homes, which were originally in short supply. Nursing homes have been increased so rapidly by public policy, with little application of criteria for determining need, that today they contain almost as many beds as general hospitals and in some areas are in oversupply.

4. *Poor utilization of manpower.* Manpower in health care and associated occupations is one of the nation's most rapidly growing fields of employment; it totaled 1.7 million in 1950 and is projected to rise to 5.3 million in 1975. Poor distribution, together with inadequate utilization, training, and organization, have aggravated the shortages of manpower in some areas while causing surpluses in others. Beyond some crude and increasingly doubtful ratios of professionals to population, it is not even known how many people are now needed, let alone how many would be needed under a better-organized system.[2]

2/There are wide differences in the numbers of personnel believed necessary because of variations in treatment methods, regional practice, personnel-population ratios, and appraisals of the efficiency of care.

If the United States did not import a large number of doctors, many of its medical institutions could not function as now staffed and operated. As many as 63,000 physicians (one out of five active doctors in the United States in 1970) are graduates of foreign medical schools. Many come from developing countries where their services are urgently needed. Foreign medical graduates fill one-third of the intern and resident positions in this country, and immigration of doctors has increased at a faster rate (83 per cent) than the domestic production of doctors in the last decade.[3]

With great unmet needs for dental care, the number of active non-federal dentists fell slightly from 50 to 47 per 100,000 people between 1950 and 1970. While this may indicate improvement in productivity as much as a shortage of dentists, nevertheless the number of dental assistants, hygienists, and other trained people has not increased sufficiently to meet the gap in needed dental services.

The nation faces a nursing shortage, aggravated by the large number of licensed nurses not actively engaged in nursing.[4] The projected increase in the proportion of older people in our population clearly indicates that there will be increasing demands for nurses in the future. Furthermore, nurses have become logical candidates for training as physician assistants and physician associates. Hence, the development of health-maintenance programs, new primary-care teams, and new modes of delivery will unquestionably put further pressure on the present supply of nurses, though in the long run these new systems will mean better utilization of nurses and generally of all health personnel.

The Fragmented System

Health care today most often takes the form of a visit by a patient to a "solo" practitioner, a doctor in practice by himself. Three-quarters of nonfederal physicians engaged in patient care are in office-based practice. Of the 140,000 offices maintained by physicians in 1970, no less than 116,000 were devoted to the practice of a single physician. Of the remainder, 13,000 offices were maintained by two doctors and 11,000 by various groupings and expense-sharing cooperative arrangements.

3/Thomas D. Dublin, "The Migration of Physicians to the United States," *New England Journal of Medicine,* Vol. 286, No. 16 (April 20, 1972), pp. 870-877.
4/An inventory by the American Nurses' Association in 1966 revealed that 286,000 qualified nurses were not employed in nursing compared with 594,000 who were.

The solo practitioner, although backed up by consultation with other doctors, by laboratories, and by his hospital, operates so small an enterprise that its very size may militate against efficiency. In many cases, it reduces his ability to provide the best of care for the diversified needs of his patients. The linkages among physicians are loosely structured, inconvenient to many patients, susceptible to episodic rather than continuous care, very often inefficient and expensive, and relatively difficult to maintain. Moreover, the burdens upon the average physician are often so great that they limit his time and narrow his perspective in keeping abreast of both medical advances and social change.

The solo practice of medicine developed at a time when the principal problems in medicine were episodic and could usually be met by the small entrepreneurship of the single physician. This is no longer true because of the growing incidence of chronic illness, the overwhelming movement toward specialization, the greater need to manage medical practice, and the desire for a health-care system that goes beyond mere medical attendance.

Nonetheless, solo practice has been highly tenacious; it is preferred by many physicians and is the form of treatment with which most people are acquainted. Moreover, many doctors are highly dedicated in discharging their vital responsibilities and today most are well-trained. The problem is that the size of their firms greatly limits their ability to provide a convenient and well-rounded health service.

The burden of securing the required health care rests with the patient. More often than not, the individual must find his own way among the various types and levels of service, with only partial help from the provider. In the majority of cases, no one in the medical profession takes responsibility for determining the appropriate level of total care needed and for seeing that such care (but no more) is supplied. Not only does this "nonsystem" lead to great variations in the quality of care rendered, but it also fails to deliver the comprehensive and preventive care now desired.

Physicians are chosen for a variety of reasons, including the nature of the ailment, proximity, professionalism, and price. For those seeking medical care, each of these considerations plays only a part, and there are variations in the weight attached to each. Price may be the major determinant in whether a poor person goes to a clinic or a private doctor, whereas this may not even be discussed or known beforehand by the affluent patient. Different diseases and different episodes may lead patients to different doctors and hospitals, and the results and findings simply may never get integrated into an overall assessment of the patient.

A patient may choose a doctor because of the nature of his illness at one time or a specialist of the wrong type because of a mistake in early diagnosis; he may stay with this physician in order to avoid the inconvenience and uncertainty of starting over again with another. Often the patient's resources are too limited to permit him to search for another physician even if he wanted to do so, or he may regard it as unseemly and indicative of a lack of confidence in the doctor on whose goodwill he depends. Moreover, the prevalence of one-man medical firms often impedes the free flow of patients from one practitioner to another; such firms run some risk of losing the referred patient to the consultant or the hospital.

Although medical care is only one factor contributing to health, it can be a matter of life and death. Self-denial because of low income is not the same in this situation as in rationing one's income when purchasing cars, clothes, or television sets. Medical costs can claim an excessive share of a family's income, even for middle-income people, who usually have insurance. The position of the consumer in the health-care marketplace is indeed an insecure and limited one. In purchasing other goods and services the consumer can police the market by shopping around, but this applies far less to medical services. The average consumer knows less about the medical service than almost any other service he pays for.

Fee-for-Service

There are several ways of paying for health care—per service, per visit, per session, per person under treatment. Doctors in particular, but other providers as well, adhere largely to one type of payment: the requirement of a specific fee for each service rendered.

This has resulted in substantial inequities in the charges made by various medical specialists.* In grave illnesses the unpredictability of needs causes a piling up of fees, and sometimes this happens with minor but chronic conditions. Even average families can wind up paying hundreds of different bills for separate X rays, tests, fillings, extractions, prescriptions, etc., and these bills are often duplicated on referral to others who provide health-care service. A single hospital bill is frequently

---

*See Memorandum by MR. D. C. SEARLE, page 93.

36.

made up of a myriad of separate entries rather than a specified and predictable amount per day or per stay. Where much of a patient's care is not insured, fees can add up to a considerable burden. Likewise, it is difficult for doctors to practice good medicine when each fee has to be weighed against an accompanying charge.

Paying a separate fee for each service adds considerably to the claim work involved in health insurance and has inhibited its development. This is especially true where the individual fees are not large and where the administrative cost, relative to the cost of the specific service insured, may appear to be disproportionate. In contrast, capitation (i.e., a fixed periodic payment per person) can greatly reduce the administrative cost of insurance and make possible the coverage of additional services.

Many who have studied the existing health-care system have begun to question the fundamental logic of paying separately for each service and each visit. The Ways and Means Committee of the House of Representatives, for example, found that payment for each individual service performed often creates an economic incentive to furnish services that may not be essential and may even be unnecessary.

Fees have become better standardized and related to each other according to the degree of difficulty or amount of service provided and efforts also are being made to monitor fees. At the same time fee-for-service is being employed in some new comprehensive delivery systems, which suggests that it is likely to continue as one method of payment. However, it is essential that there be continued examination of the issues involved in payment as well as greater experimentation with other forms of payment.

The Financial Flow Through the System

When the American people spent $83.4 billion for health care in fiscal 1972, their expenditures were devoted overwhelmingly to purchasing health services and supplies (see Table 1). Some $77.3 billion, or about 92 per cent of this amount, went for these purposes, after deducting $4.1 billion for construction or improvement of physical facilities and $2 billion for the acquisition of new knowledge.

Subtracting from the $77.3 billion the cost of operating private prepayment and insurance plans and administrating government programs ($2.9 billion), the cost of government public-health activities ($2.1 billion), and expenditures by voluntary agencies for other health services ($0.5 billion) leaves a total of $71.9 billion spent for personal health care—an amount equal to nearly 86 per cent of all health expenditures in 1972.

The total amount spent for personal care was paid to the providers as follows: one-half went to hospitals and nursing homes (45 per cent and 5 per cent respectively), including the salaries of physicians and dentists on inpatient and outpatient staffs; almost one-third went for direct professional services of physicians (22 per cent), dentists (7 per cent), and others (2 per cent); and the remainder was spent for drugs (11 per cent), eyeglasses and appliances (3 per cent), and other health services (4 per cent).

Well over half the American health industry operates within the private sector of the economy. Even after Medicare and Medicaid expanded considerably the public sector, private sources still accounted for 61 per cent of total health expenditure in fiscal 1972 and 63 per cent of the personal health expenditures. The public sources are increasingly federal. While state and local governments' share of national health expenditures rose only from 12.9 per cent to 13.5 per cent between fiscal 1966 and 1972, the federal portion doubled during these years—from 12.8 per cent to 25.8 per cent.

There are two income sources for the health system (see Figure 4). Individuals and families provide funds by purchasing services directly; by paying taxes to federal, state, and local governments; by paying health-insurance premiums; and to a lesser extent by contributing to charities. Employers are the system's only other source of income. Firms pay the employees' share of payroll taxes, make contributions for health-insurance premiums, and, of course, pay corporate income taxes. In addition, they collect taxes and premiums from their employees and pass them on to the government and private financial intermediaries. The financial intermediaries in the system are private insurers, government, and other third parties that receive funds from the two income sources described above and also purchase (or reimburse individuals who purchase) health services.

Insurance, both private and public, has become the major form of financing, accounting for some $27.4 billion of the $71.9 billion spent for personal health care. Of this amount, $19.0 billion was paid through private insurance and prepayment plans, and another $8.4 billion was paid as health insurance for the aged (Medicare).

Table One: National Health Expenditures, by Type of Expenditure and Source of Funds, Fiscal Year 1972 (in millions)

Type of Expenditure	Total	Private			Public		
		Total	Consumers	Other	Total	Federal	State and Local
TOTAL	$83,417	$50,560	$46,170	$4,390	$32,857	$21,560	$11,297
Health services and supplies	77,291	47,665	46,170	1,495	29,625	19,207	10,418
Hospital care	32,460	15,267	14,480	427	17,193	11,220	5,973
Physicians' services	16,150	12,430	12,419	11	3,720	2,803	916
Dentists' services	5,025	4,771	4,771	—	254	165	90
Other professional services	1,655	1,427	1,395	32	228	166	62
Drugs and drug sundries[1]	7,909	7,340	7,340	—	569	303	266
Eyeglasses and appliances	2,037	1,960	1,960	—	77	44	34
Nursing-home care	3,500	1,370	1,345	25	2,130	1,282	848
Expenses for prepayment and administration	2,868	2,100	2,100	—	768	638	130
Government public health activities	2,100	—	—	—	2,100	823	1,276
Other health services	3,587	1,000	—	1,000	2,587	1,763	824
Research and medical-facilities construction	6,127	2,895	—	2,895	3,232	2,353	879
Research[1]	2,029	195	—	195	1,834	1,755	79
Construction	4,098	2,700	—	2,700	1,398	598	800
Publicly owned facilities	1,052	—	—	—	1,052	266	786
Privately owned facilities	3,046	2,700	—	2,700	346	332	14

Source of Funds

1/Research expenditure of drug companies included in expenditures for drugs and drug sundries and excluded from research expenditures.

Source: U. S. Social Security Administration, *Research and Statistics Note*, No. 19 (November 29, 1972), p. 3.

Of the $71.9 billion spent in fiscal 1972 for personal health care, the direct payments of individuals constituted 34.9 per cent.[5] The remaining 65.1 per cent of the financing burden was provided indirectly: 26.4 per cent from a variety of group and individual insurance plans, 24.7 per cent from federal general revenues, 12.5 per cent from state and local taxes, and some 1.4 per cent from philanthropy and industry.

The Effects of the Financing System

The health-care financial system clearly has not functioned well in distributing the burden of expenditures among individuals or in allocating resources for various services according to need.

While most people are covered by some form of health-care insurance, there are notable gaps in the insurance system that leave large numbers of people with either inadequate coverage or no protection at all (see Chapter 5). Moreover, where there is coverage, it modifies significantly the behavior of the patient and provider in the health-care marketplace. The amount paid by the patient at point of care is a residue after the insurance or government payment. These payments reduce the price paid by the consumer relative to the price charged by the provider; this tends to increase demand for services, particularly those paid for by third parties. (This reduction is largest in the case of hospital and surgical care and almost nonexistent for preventive care.) The increased demand may not be directly due to the consumer, since the decision to seek medical care is frequently made *for* the consumer *by* the provider.

The increases in insurance and government coverage have acted in part not to replace personal expenditures for health care but to add to them. Between fiscal years 1965 and 1972 private insurance benefits increased from $8.3 to $19.0 billion and public expenditures on personal health care rose from $7.0 to $24.7 billion; meanwhile, direct individual payments also rose from $17.6 to $25.1 billion.

Of the total increase in personal health-care expenditures from fiscal years 1965 to 1972, 10 per cent is attributed to population growth

---

5/There are some inevitable weaknesses in these data; they include expenditures for all drugs (aspirin, corn removers, and vitamins) as well as some botanical and veterinary products. However, the data quality for health expenditures is no worse and, in fact, may be substantially better than it is in other social fields. Another inevitable difficulty is double counting. For example, should federal grants to state governments be counted as federal or as state expenditures? How about private spending of Medicare funds? They are treated here as federal expenditures.

Figure 5: Per Capita Expenditures for Health Care, Selected Items, Fiscal Years 1950-1972

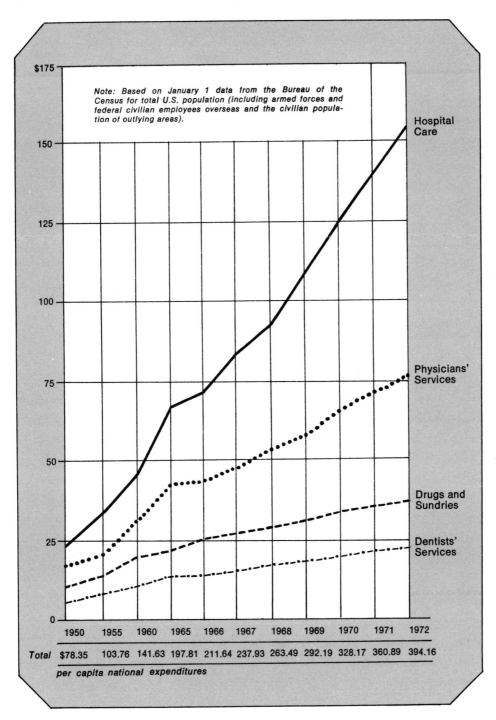

Note: Based on January 1 data from the Bureau of the Census for total U.S. population (including armed forces and federal civilian employees overseas and the civilian population of outlying areas).

Hospital Care

Physicians' Services

Drugs and Sundries

Dentists' Services

	1950	1955	1960	1965	1966	1967	1968	1969	1970	1971	1972
Total	$78.35	103.76	141.63	197.81	211.64	237.93	263.49	292.19	328.17	360.89	394.16

per capita national expenditures

Sources: U. S. Social Security Administration, *Social Security Bulletin*, Vol. 35, No. 1 (January 1972), p. 12. Revised data for 1969-1971 and newly released data for 1972 were obtained from U. S. Social Security Administration, Office of Research and Statistics.

and 38 per cent to increased per capita utilization of care combined with the rising level and scope of services resulting from innovation (e.g., new techniques, new drugs, and improved procedures for treatment). The largest share of the increase, about 52 per cent, resulted from price rises.[6] The inflationary rate in medical services has outrun the inflationary rate of consumer prices generally as reflected in the consumer price index (see Figure 6, page 43).

Utilization and prices for health care typically have risen with additions to resources. When extra personnel or equipment are added, whether they are needed or not, utilization adjusts to the increase in resources, and the fees and charges rise accordingly; insurance and government payments follow suit. An excess of surgeons, for example, does not bring down the fees for surgery. On the contrary, in the four years through 1971, the prices charged increased by about 25 per cent for the two surgical procedures—a herniorrhaphy and a tonsillectomy and adenoidectomy—that are monitored by the consumer price index. When ordinary housing is overbuilt there may be vacancies and cost concessions, but when hospitals are overbuilt the cost of hospitalization has not gone down.

While it is evident that medical manpower should be increased selectively, to be really effective the increases must be associated with reorganization of the health-care system. In the chapters that follow we explore the means for restructuring and redeploying the delivery system, creating a national insurance system that will reinforce these changes, and developing an effective planning and control structure.

Until the providers of care work within a system which requires them to respond to effective planning that meets national needs and to become involved in the consequences of their decisions, costs cannot be controlled and the system cannot be rationalized. Such an involvement is now being sought in new forms of organization and new methods of reimbursement that would require providers of health care to share in the risk.

We believe that insurers and providers will adapt responsibly to more effective planning and can become instruments for needed reforms. We feel that they should be given a fair opportunity to demonstrate their great and underutilized capacity for service under a comprehensive and planned system of health care such as that proposed in this statement.

6/U.S. Social Security Administration, *Social Security Bulletin*, Vol. 35, No. 1 (January 1972), pp. 5, 9; and idem, *Research and Statistics Note*, No. 19 (November 29, 1972), p. 2.

Figure 6: Price Indices for Selected Health-Care Items and All Consumer Items, 1950-1971 (1967=100)

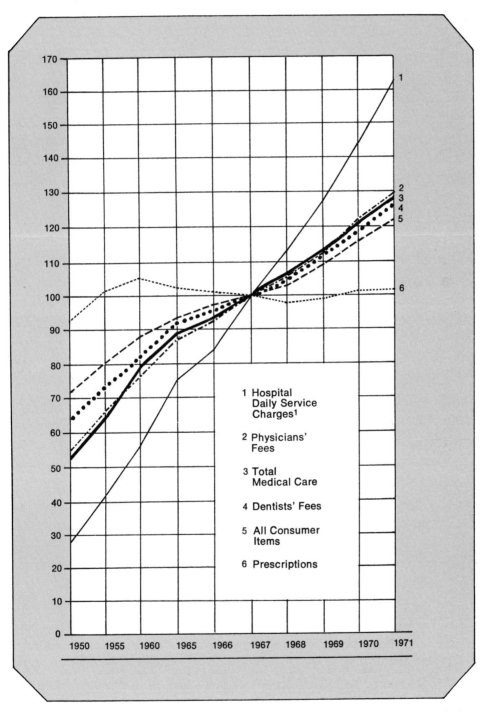

1/Includes charges to adult inpatients paying full rates for room and board, routine nursing care, and minor medical and surgical supplies.
Source: U. S. Social Security Administration, *Social Security Bulletin,* Vol. 35, No. 1 (January 1972), pp. 63, 64.

Figure 7:
Multiphasic Screening: A New Medical Subsystem

Below are extracts from a computer print-out of a multiphasic health test. This program utilizes automated technology and teams of allied health professionals to make periodic health checkups. Significant findings from a battery of tests and the health "inventory" of the patient are highlighted for the physician.

```
                                           ▬▬▬▬▬▬

                                        AGE  67
EXAM DATE  09/23/72                     SEX MALE      RACE WHITE
                                        OCCUPATION   SHIPPING-CLERK

     THIS SCREENEE HAS POSITIVE RESPONSES IN THE FOLLOWING SYSTEMS -
GENERAL, RESPIRATORY AND CARDIO-VASCULAR,
NEUROLOGICAL - PSYCHIATRIC AND SPECIAL SENSES.

     ABNORMAL RESULTS WERE FOUND IN THE FOLLOWING - EKG, CHEST X-RAY,
VISUAL ACUITY, SPIROMETRY.

REVIEW OF SYSTEMS

     GENERAL

          INSOMNIA - FIRST NOTED WITHIN PAST 6 MONTHS

          DENIED - MARKED FATIGUE, SIGNIFICANT WEIGHT LOSS


     RESPIRATORY AND CARDIO-VASCULAR

          SYNCOPE - LAST NOTED MORE THAN SIX MONTHS AGO

FAMILY HEALTH HISTORY

     RHEUMATIC HEART DISEASE                     SISTER

     DIABETES                                    SISTER

     MOTHER DIED AT AGE OF  93  DUE  TO  OLD  AGE

     FATHER DIED AT AGE OF  92  DUE  TO  OLD  AGE

HEIGHT   66.0 INCHES
WEIGHT   140 POUNDS

BLOOD PRESSURE
     RIGHT ARM  114/  82

CHEST X-RAY
     CARDIAC ENLARGEMENT

AUDIOMETRY
     RIGHT EAR
          FREQUENCIES AT   500  CPS   1000  CPS   2000  CPS   3000 CPS
                            30          40          30          60

     LEFT EAR
          FREQUENCIES AT   500  CPS   1000  CPS   2000  CPS   3000  CPS
                            40          40          40          60

HEMATOLOGY                     (NORMAL RANGES IN PARENTHESIS)

          WBC  (4900-10,500)             6,100
          HGB  (12.6-16.1)               15.4

URINALYSIS
          PH          5
          GLUCOSE     NEG
          ACETONE     NEG
          PROTEIN     NEG
          BLOOD       NEG
```

Chapter Three

Approaches
to Improving the Organization
of Delivery

Various efforts have been made through both private and public initiative to improve the nation's health-care delivery system. For many years it was assumed that the hospital would play the central role in organizing a health-care system. A quite different concept for the organization of care took the form of group practice of physicians. In the last decade, concern with the need to apply new knowledge to medical practice led to government financing of regional medical-research and demonstration centers. More recently there has been an emphasis on making health services more accessible to people through ambulatory and neighborhood health centers and bringing the mentally ill out of isolation into community centers.

Although these efforts do not provide an adequate basis for a complete and integrated delivery system, they have yielded valuable components and experience for building such a system. Above all, they affirm the need for building integrated systems and subsystems that can utilize and integrate such innovations in delivery as intensive-care units, organized home care, extended care, new communications systems, computerization of medical records and activities, and health screening programs (see Figure 7).

The Role of the Hospital

As the most highly organized component in the delivery of health care, hospitals have remained at the core of many proposals for new delivery systems even when little progress has been made in converting them to this role. Indeed, hospitals have tended to move in the opposite direction—toward more specialized services rather than toward community-based care—with the result, for example, that more hospitals have facilities for cobalt therapy and open-heart surgery than for extended care or self-care.[1] Too much may have been asked of hospitals, which have been under many conflicting pressures from diverse interests at the same time that they have been subject to few hard criteria of public need.

More than 7,000 hospitals, employing nearly 3 million people, treat some 1.4 million inpatients on an average day. Use has grown steadily from a rate of 111 admissions per 1,000 people to community hospitals in 1950 to a rate of 149 in 1971. Hospitals serve as the base for training nearly 100,000 interns, residents, and other trainees. They likewise have become a focal point of the growing centralization of medical practice; increasingly, doctors prefer the backup of the hospital's resources for sophisticated diagnosis and treatment and locate their practices in closer proximity to hospitals.

Hospitals have encouraged and sponsored the development of prepayment and insurance funds, and they have received a large share of these funds. But the concentration of prepayment and insurance on the hospital has tended to overstimulate the use of expensive inpatient care, taxing its facilities and escalating costs. One of the major impediments to efficiency in hospitals has been reimbursement of cost, which reduces incentive for economic operation. Hospital charges have been at the center of rising health costs. As the largest single item of health expenditure, the per capita cost of hospital care in fiscal 1972 of $153 was slightly larger than the *total* per capita expenditure on health in 1960. We believe that no institution can long sustain annual increases in per diem costs in the range of 12 to 16 per cent without severe consequences.

Although there has been a steady growth of personnel, the hospital suffers severe manpower shortages, at least as personnel are now used. The management of hospitals has improved with professionalization of

---

1/American Institute of Architects, *To Facilitate Health: A Proposal to Establish Health Facilities Research, Inc.,* by William F. Maloney, Jerome Pollack, and Hermann H. Field (Boston: November 15, 1971), p. 26. This study was commissioned by the Task Force on a Health Facilities Laboratory of the A.I.A.

administration and upgrading in the quality of employees. Yet fundamental problems remain unsolved in organizational structure, management, and productivity. There is a lack of clear jurisdiction among the board of trustees, medical staff, and hospital administration. Hospitals are pulled in different directions by the needs and desires of medical staffs; the aspirations of trustees; the expectations of the community; the requirements of education programs, codes, and accrediting agencies; and the demands of employees for wages and benefits. Efforts to respond to these pressures have contributed greatly to the imbalance of facilities and services as well as to rising costs.

The time has come for a searching review of the institution's mission, size, structure, and management. This should start with a re-examination of the board itself, its functions, powers, and composition. The member who spends one luncheon a month with the hospital board cannot possibly learn enough about the workings of the hospital to do anything more than rubber-stamp the administrator and the medical staff. Greater participation of people with interest and experience, who know how to manage institutions and who are willing to speak up even at the risk of offending, can greatly improve the hospital. Of equal importance is the appropriate involvement of the medical staff with the hospital's budget and operations. There should be clear assignment of administrative authority to assure that the hospital is run according to an operating plan.

Steps must be taken to improve the efficiency of hospitals; to moderate rising costs, which have been passed on through carriers to consumers; and to bring hospitals into full participation with new delivery systems. Many of these steps have been identified and are now well known, albeit they are more honored than practiced. Governor Rockefeller's Committee on Hospital Costs, chaired by Marion B. Folsom, made a series of such recommendations with which we strongly concur.[2] These include:

■ Rounding out planning networks so that all hospitals are involved in effective planning and every locality has a strong planning agency concerned with health needs and facilities;

■ Converting underutilized beds to other needed uses before expansion of a hospital is permitted;

■ Encouraging full operation of hospitals on weekends;

2/New York State. Governor's Committee on Hospital Costs, *Summary of Findings and Recommendations* (1965).

- Consolidating some hospitals, converting others to different kinds of uses, and closing those that are unnecessary;
- Making utilization procedures function as a requirement of all insurance plans and providing external as well as internal review;
- Strengthening hospital management by exchange of data and by providing technical assistance to aid hospitals in solving management problems;
- Improving statistical reporting by establishing uniform categories and definitions;
- Expanding existing programs of grants and loans to replenish facilities and build needed new types;
- Establishing cost incentives that put the hospital at risk.

The hospital has a central role in any health-care system. The degree to which it may involve itself in the organization of that system is dependent on its success in internal restructuring and its acceptance of and participation in community programs. Although we believe that each hospital has an individual responsibility for bringing about many of the needed reforms, it is clear that some of them cannot be accomplished without concerted or group action by hospitals generally. This, in turn, cannot be assured without public review and planning. Our recommendations on strengthened planning and review mechanisms to accomplish this formidable and urgent task with respect to hospitals and other health facilities appear in Chapter 6.

The Evolution of Group Practice

Another framework for organizing health services is group practice, which is finally gaining greater acceptance by physicians after a slow start. According to surveys, the number of groups increased from 1,550 in 1959, to 4,300 in 1965, and to 6,200 in 1969. The number of physicians practicing in groups increased from 28,400 in 1965 to 40,000 in 1969, or about one out of five of all U.S. doctors engaged in patient care.[3] This reflects the growing awareness in the profession of the advantages to be gained by sharing such resources as laboratories, sophisticated technology, technicians, nurses, secretaries, receptionists, and

---

3/Clifford Todd and Mary Elaine McNamara, *Medical Groups in the U.S., 1969* (Chicago: American Medical Association, 1971), pp. 74, 78.

bookkeepers. These increase the effectiveness and efficiency of the practitioner's services at the same time they give him the chance to practice a more contemporary form of medicine and to enjoy a more satisfactory mode of life.

Thus far, however, the results of group practice for the patient have not been as impressive as the advantages enjoyed by the group; frequently the patients do not receive the benefits of reduced medical costs. Many groups have been drawn together by their professional, economic, and intellectual interests rather than by a desire to meet the diversified needs of the clientele. Of the 6,400 groups existing in 1969, only slightly more than a third provided multispecialty care, one-half were devoted to a single specialty, and the remainder were in general practice. A minority of the groups (about a fifth) were hospital-based, and only 385 groups were directly associated with prepayment and offering care to a subscribing population.

The full advantages to the patient are realized when group practice is linked with prepayment and thus associated with a subscribing population or clientele. Prepaid comprehensive group care is not new; its beginnings trace back to the Community Hospital of Elk City, Oklahoma, in the late 1920s. Several plans have developed into large-scale operations, in part through the stimulus of consumer groups, labor unions, and government employees. In 1970, the Kaiser Foundation Health Plans of Northern and Southern California and Oregon had 962,000, 900,000, and 145,000 members respectively; the Health Insurance Plan of Greater New York, 780,000; Group Health Cooperative of Puget Sound, 136,-000; and Group Health Association of the District of Columbia, 75,500. Approximately 7 million people are now covered by such prepayment plans. Prepaid comprehensive health-care organization is described more fully in Chapter 4.

Other kinds of groupings have also come into being, notably the foundation plan initiated by medical societies. Starting in 1954 with the San Joaquin County Foundation for Medical Care, organizations of physicians have undertaken to review the utilization of care, to monitor insurance claims, and to set criteria for benefits and fees. These foundations, which are technically autonomous from the medical societies, have spread to some thirty-five areas. In a number of instances they have provided a structure for linking the individual practices of physicians and providing hospital- or health-insurance coverage. These and other foundation plans now in process of formation have the possibility of conversion into a form of health-maintenance organization.

49.

Decentralized Approaches

Within the decade there has been a significant shift in the way that the nation's health problems are perceived and in the institutional response to the problems. In the early 1960s there was enormous concern with the application to medicine of rapidly accumulating new knowledge; this led the President's Commission on Heart Disease, Cancer and Stroke to propose a massive increase in research and training through a national network of regional centers. These government-sponsored regional medical programs have suffered from flaws in concept, inadequate recognition of the requisites of effective planning, and exaggerated expectations of the initiative of the large medical centers.

The emphasis has since shifted to more direct ways of getting care to people. This has led to experimentation with innovative, decentralized units that reach into neighborhoods where the need for services is acute. These emerging forms of delivery can become vitally important components of an integrated health-care system. Several major types can be identified.

Ambulatory-care centers enable physicians to perform more effectively in providing primary care where it is needed through the assistance of trained teams. The new physician assistants are accepted by patients, and function at lower cost than that of physicians. Recent experiments also show that such centers, properly equipped and staffed, could perform 20 to 25 per cent of all the surgery now done on a costly in-patient basis in hospitals, as well as much of the diagnostic X-ray and laboratory testing.

There is now general agreement on the urgent need to strengthen ambulatory care. The Health Insurance Association of America believes it should be made accessible in every community, while the American Hospital Association finds in it a significant shift to "the philosophy of keeping people out of health-care institutions."[4] With the addition of community-based health services—such as home care, social service, well-baby clinics, and mental-health clinics—the ambulatory-care center could become the key element in health maintenance.

Neighborhood health centers, which provide a broader array of services than ambulatory-care centers, have materially improved the

---

4/Health Insurance Association of America, *Program for Healthcare in the 1970's* (Washington, D. C.: 1970), p. 8; and American Hospital Association, *Report of a Special Committee on the Provision of Health Services: Ameriplan—A Proposal for the Delivery and Financing of Health Services in the United States* (Chicago: 1970), p. 52.

organization of health care in deprived areas. Their staffs include social workers, public-health personnel, and others who can provide various forms of assistance through social and governmental agencies. They have reached out to neighborhoods, responding to the health conditions of their constituencies. They also serve as a desirable initial point of entry into a health-care system, and they could be employed effectively to route patients to all components of a comprehensive health-care system. The neighborhood health centers have made a start toward a system of health care rather than medical care.

A great handicap to the functioning of both ambulatory-care and neighborhood health centers has been their uncertain funding of both capital and operating costs. Support has to be solicited from many different sources, local, state, and federal; funding is frequently not related to the requirements of these centers. It has been observed that to sustain an integrated program often requires "heroic effort."[5] There is widespread agreement that ambulatory- and preventive-care benefits should be included in all health-insurance plans.

A Breakthrough in Mental-Health Services

More than a million people have mental and nervous conditions causing limitation of activity. Mental problems are the fourth most prevalent cause of disabling chronic conditions, following heart conditions, impairments, arthritis and rheumatism. About a tenth of total health-care manpower is engaged in mental-health services. There are some 23,000 psychiatrists, 16,000 psychologists who work in mental health, and 33,000 psychiatric nurses. It has been estimated that the cost of treating and preventing mental illness in the United States was slightly more than $4 billion in 1968, or about $20 per capita. Forty-three per cent of this cost was borne by state and local governments, 25 per cent by the federal government, 18 per cent by patients and their families, 12 per cent by private insurance, and the remaining 2 per cent by private industry and philanthropy.[6]

There has been remarkable transformation in the delivery of mental-health services since the mid-1950s, when tranquilizers were introduced as the first in a series of new modes of therapy. Between 1950

5/Leonard S. Rosenfeld, *Ambulatory Care: Planning and Organization* (Rockville, Md.: Health Services and Mental Health Administration, 1971).
6/Louis S. Reed, Evelyn S. Myers, and Patricia L. Scheidemandel, *Health Insurance and Psychiatric Care* (Washington, D. C.: American Psychiatric Association, 1972), p. 40.

and 1970, the number of patients residing in mental-health institutions dropped from 560,000 to 340,000—a decrease of about 40 per cent when an increase of the same magnitude might otherwise have been expected. In the 1960s, beds in psychiatric hospitals decreased from 722,000 to 527,000, while the number of admissions rose from 360,000 to 600,000, as short-term treatment dramatically took hold. At the same time, psychiatric outpatient visits increased from 892,000 in 1962 to 2.7 million in 1970.

What has occurred has been a productive congruence of scientific advance, new techniques in treatment, organizational restructuring, relatively ample funding, and supportive social policy. In twenty years, mental-health treatment has moved from reliance on individual psycho-therapy and shock treatment to a multimodal specialty that can treat effectively the large majority of patients. These new treatments include not only psychotropic medications but also group therapy, therapeutic community treatment, and behavioral therapy. Furthermore, a creative approach to facilities and new groupings of professionals and parapro-fessionals has accompanied these advances and contributed to their effective utilization. In particular, the Community Mental Health Center program of the National Institutes of Mental Health has helped to bring into being a comprehensive delivery system at decentralized sites near people's homes.

Mental-health care thus has been liberated from the barren practices of custodial care in isolation. The community and team approaches, day care, and the change from the traditional one-to-one relationship have resulted in a twenty-four-hour-a-day therapeutic experience for the patient. Since this likewise has meant more efficient use of the physician's time, the new techniques have been shown to be cost-effective. Such mental-health delivery systems can serve as an innovative model worthy of examination by the health field generally.*

It should be noted that the community mental-health centers were established separately because there was no way to bring them into a single system for comprehensive community-based care. The result is a separate set of programs, different in sponsorship and areas from the medical delivery system. This may cause difficulty when the attempt is made eventually to reconcile mental-health services with a comprehensive health-care system. A further difficulty with these centers, as in the case of those providing general ambulatory and neighborhood services, is inadequate financing of their programs over the long term.

*See Memorandum by MR. D. C. SEARLE, page 94.

Basic to the establishment of a national health-care system is a determined and adequately supported program to make health services more accessible to people, all of whom will be entitled to receive basic benefits. Specifically, this will require a greatly accelerated development of ambulatory- and primary-care centers, particularly in areas of special need; mental-health centers; and especially organizations that assume responsibility for providing comprehensive and continuous care. We recommend that federal grants and loan guarantees be extended to encourage private and public construction of such agencies and activities, as certified by the appropriate health-planning agencies and authorized by the Secretary of Health, Education, and Welfare. Also of vital importance is the continuous financing of such services, through a national system that we propose, and the integration of components into a comprehensive program of health care in each region.

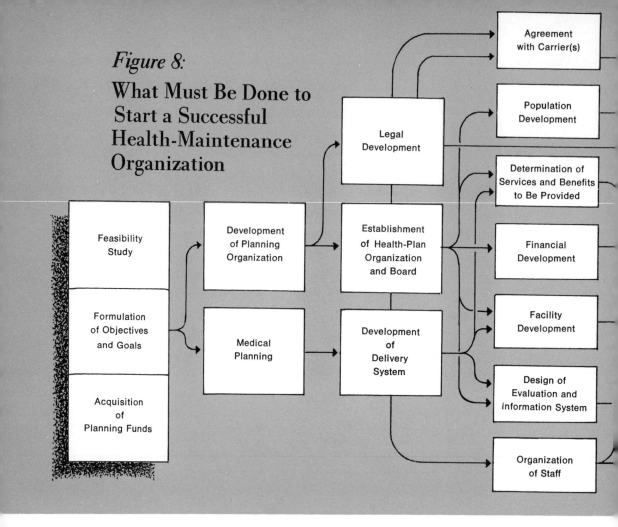

Figure 8:

What Must Be Done to Start a Successful Health-Maintenance Organization

Feasibility Study	Development of Planning Organization	Legal Development	Agreement with Carrier(s)
Formulation of Objectives and Goals	Medical Planning	Establishment of Health-Plan Organization and Board	Population Development
Acquisition of Planning Funds		Development of Delivery System	Determination of Services and Benefits to Be Provided
			Financial Development
			Facility Development
			Design of Evaluation and Information System
			Organization of Staff

Chapter Four

Toward an Integrated System: Prepaid Comprehensive Care

What kind of system can provide a framework to integrate the functions of health care and respond most effectively to the unmet needs of the present and the new demands of the future?

Such a system must provide care that is personal, comprehensive, and continuous. It must be dedicated to serve the health needs of its

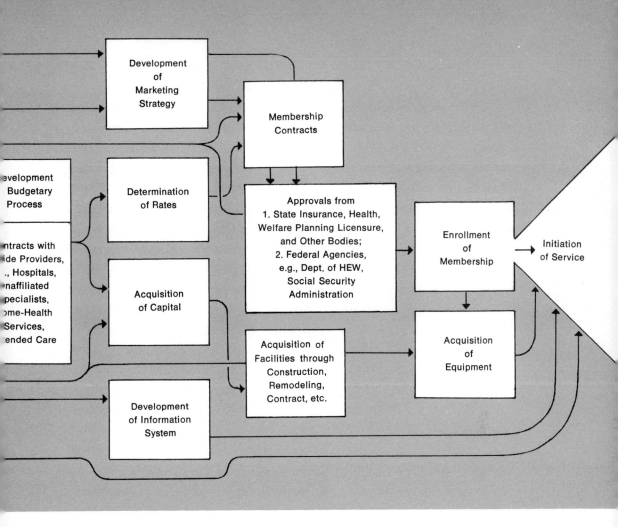

subscribers and deployed in such a way as to be readily available to them. It must have incentives for efficiency, so that health-care resources are used to the fullest and rising costs restrained. It must offer satisfaction to doctors seeking to practice in close collaboration with their colleagues and to employ more fully the new technologies of medicine. To assure the quality of care, a network of responsibility must be established throughout the system. Finally, there must be a firm linking of both the financing and the delivery systems.

The objectives of health care often have been cast in passive terms of providing more medical treatment for those who present themselves. A health-delivery system must be more affirmative and dynamic; it must seek out the untreated and encourage them to use the resources that are available. In reorganizing the nation's health-care services it is important to move beyond mere medical attendance into a positive system of health care.

To achieve a national health-care system that stresses prevention as well as cure, we recommend (1) that financing be based on prepayment for an essential set of benefits, and (2) that to the maximum feasible extent providers of care be paid in accordance with fees and charges fixed in advance by agreement with providers and related to a budget that reflects efficient organization and procedure. We believe that the application of the concept of the health-maintenance organization represents an admirable and efficient response to such a payment system. *

The health-maintenance organization (HMO) is based on prepayment and undertakes relatively complete and continuous care for a subscribing clientele or population. Among the many accomplishments of existing health-maintenance organizations are striking reductions in the utilization of inpatient care (see Table 2), as well as improved use of manpower and more complete care at an economical cost to subscribers. These achievements have led to the current efforts by Congress, the Administration, and private parties to develop health-maintenance organizations on a much larger scale.[1]

Comprehensive prepaid plans have brought the operations of a market in health care closer to need and have also brought more competition into health services. We see these new organizations as operating side by side and competing with conventional practice with the intent of improving the operations of both systems. The health-maintenance organization can thus serve a vital role in strengthening the present delivery system and stimulating its reform. **

Although group-practice prepayment has inspired and stimulated the HMO, it constitutes only one such kind of organization. In order to broaden the base for development and to stimulate innovation in organizational design, diverse sponsorship should be encouraged. Many of the nation's 7,000 hospitals could develop or participate in health-maintenance organizations. Potentially, any of the 6,000 existing medical groups now without prepayment plans could convert into health-maintenance organizations. As noted earlier, another prospect is the foundation for medical care, a plan actively advanced by many physicians.

1/Health-care organizations of the kind just described are proposed in several forms under different names. The Administration is promoting Health Maintenance Organizations (HMOs); the American Hospital Association is backing Health Care Corporations (HCCs); the Kennedy-Griffiths bill advances Comprehensive Health Services Organizations (CHSOs). These differ somewhat. The Kennedy-Griffiths bill, for example, leans toward nonprofit group practice or similar arrangements, whereas the Administration invites a wider range of innovative delivery systems and would include proprietary as well as nonprofit plans. By the same token, HCCs would appear to be more highly structured than HMOs.

*See Memorandum by MR. ROBERT T. FOOTE, page 91.
**See Memorandum by MR. WAYNE E. THOMPSON, page 90.

Table Two: Hospital Use Under Different Types of Plans

Hospital Days* per Thousand Persons Covered
by the Federal Employees Benefits Program

	1962	1964	1968
1. BLUE CROSS—BLUE SHIELD	882	919	924
2. INSURANCE	760	949	987
3. GROUP PRACTICE PLANS	460	453	422
Selected Plans:			
Group Health Association, District of Columbia	462	484	363
Health Insurance Plan of Greater New York	483	612	459
Group Health Cooperative of Puget Sound, Seattle, Washington	372	467	364
Kaiser Foundation Health Plan, Oregon Region	350	475	254
Kaiser Foundation Health Plan, Northern California Region	500	474	468
Kaiser Foundation Health Plan, Southern California Region	378	381	428
Kaiser Foundation Health Plan, Hawaii Region	705	522	357
4. INDIVIDUAL PRACTICE PLANS	538	530	471
Selected Plans:			
Foundation for Medical Care of San Joaquin County, California	458	578	390
Group Health Insurance, New York	547	673	652
Hawaii Medical Service Association	535	483	433
Seguros de Servicio de Salud de Puerto Rico	658	644	553
Washington Physicians Service, District of Columbia	531	523	438

*Does not include maternity days.

Source: U. S. Health Services and Mental Health Administration, *The Federal Employees Health Benefits Program* (1971), p. 11.

Occupational-health programs within the offices and plants of commerce and industry (where as many as 7 million visits are paid annually) might be converted into general HMOs, as in the case of the Kaiser Foundation Health Plan. Consumer and community groups, as well as labor unions, have sponsored HMOs. Insurance companies and Blue Cross-Blue Shield are now actively developing such organizations. Academic institutions also have formed plans; among new plans in operation are those involving medical schools at Johns Hopkins, Harvard, and Yale. Other plans are being developed under varied sponsorship in a number of places, including Minneapolis and St. Paul, Albuquerque, and Rochester (N.Y.)

In order to engage the maximum resources and enlist the broadest possible support, diversity in the sponsorship and format of health-maintenance organizations should be encouraged. In the framing of supporting legislation, room should be made for both profit and nonprofit health-care plans sponsored by all types of organizations that can qualify in terms of capability and responsibility. In providing for the delivery and financing of care, a health-maintenance organization should offer inducements and incentives for the participation of subscribers and of physicians and other personnel. Eligible subscribers should be given the opportunity to join, and members should periodically have option of leaving the plan.

Obstacles to Overcome

It is important to interject here a cautionary note. Great damage could be done to the nation's health-care system by arousing false hopes for the health-maintenance organization by promising more than it can deliver. The potentials of the HMO will not be achieved easily or immediately. To bring into being sufficient HMOs to serve large numbers of people adequately and efficiently will require intensive planning, painstaking effort, the accumulation and exchange of new data, and a willingness to learn by trial and error. There are formidable managerial, financial, and often legal hurdles to overcome in establishing a successful HMO; there is likewise the question of scale. Nor should prompt public acceptance of this relatively new and unknown form of health-care delivery be expected.

To achieve a major impact on the organization of health-care delivery a great number of plans will have to be formed, giving a large number of people the opportunity to enroll. We believe that such a program must be undertaken on a scale appropriate for a country in the process of establishing a national health-insurance system. With the pioneering efforts behind us, with accumulating knowledge of how to proceed, and with increased support, a severalfold increase can be anticipated in the number of people covered by such plans by the early 1980s. We regard this as a reasonable and attainable goal.

To accomplish this will require a determined and well supported program of innovation by carriers. In actual practice today, there is not much preventive care beyond immunizations, prenatal care, well-baby clinics, and some screening programs. The nation does not even have a tradition that emphasizes periodic checkups. Most people want therapeutic care; they are neither aware of nor are they seeking preventive care as such and may be skeptical about its effectiveness. Therefore, only a minority of the people eligible can be expected to join initially, although enrollment is likely to accelerate once there is broader acquaintanceship with the advantages of such plans.

Legal preparation for the development of prepaid health-care systems must also go forward. The present statutes did not contemplate such organizations as HMOs. Some of the enabling legislation for present prepayment plans and insurance law may not be suitable and might reduce the effectiveness or inhibit the development of HMOs. There are legislative limitations restricting the right to organize group practices to provide comprehensive care, to establish prepayment plans offering comprehensive benefits, or to combine group practice with prepayment. They may limit the right of consumers to operate such organizations, restrict the geographic scope of operations, or prevent the delegation of the physician's tasks to others, a topic examined later in this statement.

Archaic legislation and rulings impede the development of new comprehensive delivery systems. We endorse efforts by the federal government to secure adoption of model state laws to facilitate the formation and operation of such organizations and urge that the states adopt legislation supportive of HMOs. We recommend that federal support for various state health programs be predicated on the elimination of restrictive legislation impeding improvement in the organization of health care.

Organizing and Managing a Health System

Scale is an important factor in the operation of an HMO. If the plan group is not of sufficient size, it may either provide insufficient services or fail financially, or perhaps both.

Through its own resources and by contracted services, the HMO should be able to provide comprehensive care, including emergency services, on a twenty-four-hour basis. An HMO may provide hospital care through its own facilities or by contracting for inpatient-care backup services, and emergency care in existing institutions. Arrangements may also be made for nursing-home care; organized home care; rehabilitation; and other services in various homes, agencies, and centers. Provision of decentralized access to ambulatory and primary care in neighborhood-based centers would make the plan more responsive to the locality and its problems and serve as an easily available initial point of entry into the system. These centers should be able to offer the great bulk of medical services required. The hospital-based medical delivery system offers some advantages such as proximity to care at all levels and utilization of the hospital's X-ray and laboratory facilities more fully.

An HMO's basic benefits should include physician services in the office, hospital, or home; hospital services; surgical care; prenatal and postnatal care, as well as doctor and hospital services for mother and child during confinement; X-ray and laboratory services; radiotherapy; physical examinations; well-baby care; and immunizations. Benefits will need to be provided for participants requiring care outside of the HMO's normal service area or in emergencies within the area if the patient is brought to a nonparticipating physician or institution. Coverage also needs to be assured if the patient wishes to convert to other protection on leaving the area or changing employment-based group or community trusteeship.

Health-maintenance organizations should serve a cross section of the population. It would be highly undesirable to encourage and perpetuate a two-class system of health care—one system for the prosperous sector of the population and the other for the disadvantaged. Apart from the social considerations involved, this would almost inevitably produce two levels in quality. The possibilities are very real that some HMOs may compete not in performance and service but rather in enrolling favorable populations, leaving the high-cost risks to others.*

Health-maintenance organizations should develop broad benefits in keeping with their objective of preventive and maintenance roles. Beyond that, they should be encouraged to provide a larger amount of service or more types of service than the benefits that are provided in a national program. To the fullest extent possible, HMOs should serve a

---

*See Memorandum by MR. MARVIN BOWER, page 94.

cross section, both socioeconomic and racial, of people who wish to join in their areas of operation.* We recommend that, as a condition of public support, such plans serve without discrimination of any kind.

Crucial organizational and managerial decisions must be made at the very outset. For example, the functions of prepayment and delivery of care are not only different but also require separate structures, which are usually organized as two distinct though interacting entities. In small plans of a few hundred to a few thousand members, the medical group may function well despite some diseconomies of scale by drawing on highly trained professionals. But in the small plans the management and fiscal operation usually suffers, and they rarely if ever develop effectiveness in overall management, recruitment, fiscal operations, planning, and the like. The small plans would probably be much more effective if the delivery system were to be teamed up with a larger management-fiscal mechanism that is better equipped to raise funds, develop facilities, handle data, and undertake the recruitment of subscribers. This would not narrow the choices among delivery systems but should even increase their number.

As is increasingly clear, the key to the success of a health system is its management. The National Advisory Commission on Health Manpower stated the point succinctly in its 1967 report with the observation that "the Kaiser Foundation [Health Plan] has achieved real economies, while maintaining high quality of care, through a delicate interplay of managerial and professional interests. This has resulted from structuring economic arrangements so that both professional and managerial partners have a direct economic stake in the successful and efficient operation of the overall program." There has been little application to the field of health care of such managerial and administrative techniques, which are commonplace in business and industry and increasingly utilized in government. We believe that the introduction of the principles of organization and management, as illustrated in Figure 8 and described in greater detail in Appendix A, will enormously improve the functioning of any health-care system.

---

*See Memorandum by MR. MARVIN BOWER, page 92.

Table Three:
Coverage Under Private Health-Insurance Plans
Net Enrollment by Age and Type of Care, 1970

	All Ages		Under Age 65		Age 65 and over	
	Number in thousands	Percent of civilian population	Number in thousands	Percent of civilian population	Number in thousands	Percent of civilian population
HOSPITAL CARE	162,989	80.3	152,567	83.5	10,422	51.3
PHYSICIANS' SERVICES						
Surgical services	157,670	77.7	147,618	80.8	10,052	49.4
In-hospital visits	145,589	71.7	137,229	75.1	8,360	41.1
X-ray and laboratory examinations	142,441	70.2	134,839	73.8	7,602	37.4
Office and home visits	91,581	45.1	87,625	48.0	3,956	19.5
DENTAL CARE	12,210	6.0	12,079	6.6	131	.6
PRESCRIBED DRUGS						
Out of hospital	100,966	49.7	97,736	53.5	3,230	15.9
NURSING						
Private duty	100,235	49.4	97,017	53.1	3,218	15.8
Visiting nurse service	106,882	52.6	103,064	56.4	3,818	18.8
Home care	32,392	16.0	27,371	15.0	5,021	24.7
HIAA ESTIMATES						
Hospital care	181,624	89.4	170,214	93.2	11,410	56.1
Surgical services	167,850	82.7	158,406	86.7	9,444	46.4

Note: Enrollment, as of December 31, 1970.

Source: U. S. Social Security Administration, Social Security Bulletin, Vol. 35, No. 2 (February 1972), p. 4.

Chapter Five

A National Health-Insurance Program

For over a generation, the main thrust of the nation's efforts to assure people of access to health care has been the elimination of economic impediments to care by means of insurance. As a result, the vast majority of Americans have acquired some health-insurance coverage. The proportion of people under sixty-five years of age having some form of health insurance is estimated at between 84 and 93 per cent of the civilian population for 1970 (see Table 3). Medicare further moved the nation significantly toward universal insurance by extending entitlement to virtually all persons sixty-five and over.

Of the 203 million persons making up the civilian population at the end of 1970, somewhere between 20 and 40 million persons had no hospital insurance. Data released in January 1972 by the National Center for Health Statistics showed 36 million people under sixty-five without hospital insurance in 1968. If other forms of protection had been taken into account, greater gaps in coverage would have been revealed. Following is a profile of those remaining groups that chiefly lacked protection.

■ The uninsured were concentrated among the poor. As many as 64 per cent of people with family incomes of less than $3,000 and 43 per cent in families with incomes of $3,000 to $5,000 were uninsured.

■ As many as 44 per cent of nonwhites were uninsured, compared with 19 per cent of all whites.

■ Among the categories of people less often insured were the unmarried (24 per cent were not insured), the widowed (29 per cent), the divorced (30 per cent), and the separated (49 per cent).

■ People with various kinds of disabilities were also often uninsured. Among those limited in some degree by disability in pursuit of their major activity, 30 per cent of those under sixty-five were not insured. Among those unable to carry on their major activity, as many as 51 per cent were uninsured.

■ The uninsured were also often to be found among the unemployed. In many instances, even brief periods of unemployment result in a loss of protection, despite many efforts to extend coverage during interruptions of work and sustained unemployment.

■ Occupations in which coverage is relatively limited include service workers (26 per cent) and farm workers (52 per cent).

It is evident that the arrangements that have brought coverage to most other people are unlikely to reach these groups and that determined efforts will have to be made if the entire population is to be provided with health-insurance protection. However, given the present aggregate high level of coverage and the cumulative experience in developing insurance programs, this goal is attainable through improvement and extension of the present system.

We recommend enactment of a health-insurance program that would require a basic level of protection to be made available to all Americans regardless of their means, age, or other conditions. This coverage should be continuous, without interruptions during a hiatus in employment or for any other cause; treatment should not be delayed for determinations of liability for payment, and care should not be foregone or deferred because of inability to pay. First priority should be assigned to making insurance available to all for all of the benefits that can be provided promptly within the resources available on inauguration of the program. We recommend that those benefits be expanded in a phased progression geared to the availability of services, to the reorganization of the health system, to minimizing price inflation, and to achieving greater uniformity and effectiveness of coverage.*

---

*See Memorandum by MISS CATHERINE CLEARY, page 91.

To secure truly universal coverage, health insurance will have to be legally required. Government has required insurance, public and private, on a very large scale in the United States, and disputes over whether government has the right to do this have long been resolved. There is now mandated coverage of occupational injury, old-age, survivors, disability, health for the aged, unemployment, automobile liability, and temporary disability in a few jurisdictions. In addition to the humanitarian aims of such insurance, it also reduces or avoids the public cost of assistance for the afflicted.

We recommend that national health-insurance coverage be provided through a three-category system:

> **1. Employers should be required by statute to provide a minimum level of employment-based insurance protection for all employed persons and their dependents for specified basic benefits under qualified plans.**
>
> **2. Medicare would continue to cover aged persons under the social-security system and those eligible for disability benefits under both the social-security and railroad-retirement acts, with certain modifications in benefit provisions.**
>
> **3. Federally-sponsored community trusteeships should be established to assure basic benefits for all persons ineligible under the above categories. These would include the poor and near-poor, people between jobs as well as the long-term unemployed, part-time employees not qualified for employment-based plans, and the self-employed. Also covered in this category would be aliens,* the temporarily disabled, and people regarded as uninsurable by customary insurance standards to the extent practically and legally feasible. Agencies of state and local government should be able to perform the trustee role if they are qualified.**

This program would largely replace Medicaid, reducing it to a smaller, residual role. Insofar as the self-employed and others are concerned, those with sufficient resources to cover all health contingencies could satisfy the requirements through self-insurance or existing means of protection.

---

*See Memorandum by MR. MARVIN BOWER, page 92.

Phasing and Priorities

Obviously, such a system cannot, and should not, be created overnight, nor can all Americans be assured of access to care by any single act, including the enactment of national health insurance. Rather a sequence of steps is needed.

During our deliberations great stress was placed on developing a practical program that does not raise false hopes by promising services that cannot be made available and that does not lead to unwarranted increases in costs with little benefit to people. In our judgment, the balance between reasonable benefits and affordable cost can be achieved only if there is proper phasing in inaugurating and expanding any program. Otherwise the financing provisions will outrun the capabilities of the system. Progression toward a universal health system requires the careful phasing of all its major components, starting with an interim program and progressing toward one that is uniform as well as universal. Provision must be made for phasing in various features, especially benefits, that cannot be prudently provided at first. Likewise, sufficient lead time must be allowed for preparation.

Fortunately, there is already available an extensive structure on which to build. Conceived of in this way, extensive preparations have in fact been made for such a program over many years, and completion largely requires an expansion of existing structures. In our view, basic benefits could begin within two years following enactment. This is made possible by the many thousands of employment-based plans already in existence, the numerous insurance and prepayment plans operating in every area of the country, and the massive Medicare program. After the initiating phase, other benefits could be made available at reasonable intervals depending on the availability of service and the readiness of the insurance.

Priorities should be established in terms of the greatest need among people. For example, dental insurance might be extended first to the poor; in limited form it might be extended in a few years to children generally and still later to adults generally; finally, benefits could be broadened for all. Such a time scheme would foster the concurrent and orderly development of resources and improvements in the delivery system. In addition, priority should be given to the development and expansion of those vitally important types of services that are now largely uninsured, e.g., ambulatory care, organized home care, and examinations to detect and prevent disease.

Developing Benefit Standards

At the outset of the program there will be many levels of benefits under existing plans. It will be necessary to prescribe a basic set of benefits applying to all three categories. The basic standards could be progressively increased and broadened until a single high standard is established. A few precedents and principles can serve as guides for determining this standard.

Medicare was the first national effort to develop benefit standards, and its benefits are the minimum required under various proposals for health-maintenance organizations. Although Medicare benefits are tailored to some extent to the special requirements of the aged population, such as expected high use of care, they offer a basis of comparison and a possible target for standards for the general population.[1]

Another kind of benefit standard exists in the Medicaid legislation, which prescribes a set of required basic services for those eligible for assistance under the program.[2] The difficulties with Medicaid have not been in the standards adopted but rather are inherent in the attempt to use public assistance rather than insurance as the basis for assuring health care. The program fostered a two-class system of care. Likewise, it encountered the usual difficulties that confront the administration of welfare, and these are compounded in the medical field. There was little actuarial discipline. The burden of unexpected and rising costs fell with unexpected severity on state and local governments. The benefits lacked specificity and they were not uniformly applied or well administered by the states. If these defects were eliminated, however, the basic Medicaid package could serve as a minimum standard for all people.

1/Under Part A of Medicare, the benefits include (1) inpatient care in a participating hospital for up to 90 days in each benefit period; (2) care in a psychiatric hospital with a lifetime limit of 190 benefit days; (3) extended-care benefits after the patient leaves the hospital for up to 100 days in each benefit period; and (4) home health benefits after hospital discharge for up to 100 visits in each benefit period. Under Part B, to which almost all beneficiaries have subscribed, extensive supplementary benefits are offered. These include (1) medical and surgical services by a doctor of medicine or osteopa'hy; (2) specified medical and surgical services by a doctor of dental medicine, dental surgery, or by a podiatrist; (3) ambulance services; (4) hospital outpatient benefits; (5) outpatient physical therapy services; (6) home health benefits; and (7) other medical services and supplies. The benefits under both parts are subject to some copayment requirements.

2/Under Medicaid, these include inpatient and outpatient hospital services, laboratory and X-ray services, skilled nursing home services, physicians' services, diagnostic screening and treatment for people under twenty-one years, and home health services. Additional benefits that may be provided include dental services, physical therapy and related services, prescribed drugs, dentures, prosthetic devices, and eyeglasses. The level of services in any of these categories was not specified but left to determination by the states. With the mounting difficulties encountered by the Medicaid program, the benefits in many states have not reached the level and scope originally intended.

A few basic principles to guide the design of a broader national program can be drawn from experience. The scope of benefits should start with basic protection for all and progress toward comprehensive coverage. Excessive gaps in coverage and excessive out-of-pocket expenditures should be avoided. Incentives for ambulatory care and other improvements should be built in. There should be flexibility in order to allow for the orderly development of future benefits. In addition, the program should be responsive to specific populations as well as to local and regional conditions.

Protection against financial catastrophe resulting from severe or long illness—often called catastrophic coverage—should be included as a benefit. As the sole form of health insurance, catastrophic insurance is hardly adequate. But its inclusion in a comprehensive health-insurance plan is essential, even though much work remains to be done in coping with such problems as that created by borderline cases between medical and domiciliary care over long periods.

In its early stages, the national standard could include the benefits shown in Appendix B. This illustrates not only a possible standard of benefits but also the way in which such benefits might be phased in developing a comprehensive national health-insurance program.

How the Benefits
Would Be Applied and Financed

The three categories that form the basis of our proposal for a national health-insurance program would have different means of financing and, as already noted, different levels of benefits in the initial stages.

1. *Employment-based insurance.* All employers with one or more full-time employees would be required by statute to provide a plan of health insurance offering at least the basic benefits. All full-time employees, those part-time employees who fulfill a qualifying level of employment, and eligible dependents would be covered. This category of coverage includes by far the overwhelming majority of Americans. Many of the shortcomings of these plans are caused by a lack of benefit standards and of more secure financing—two flaws that would now be rectified.

In view of the diversity of present plans and the differences in principles, it will be necessary to allow latitude in applying new benefit standards. Some present plans are comprehensive and in the aggregate may exceed the prescribed basic benefit standard without conforming to certain specific provisions.

We recommend that any employer already providing benefits that in the aggregate are equivalent to or in excess of the standards, though differing in some respects from them, should be held in conformance with the required plan. Administrative procedures and criteria should be developed to determine compliance. However, after a prescribed period, all plans would be required to comply with each benefit standard in addition to overall compliance.

One serious drawback to financing through payroll contributions is that such contributions might exceed a manageable level for many employers and employees. This would occur mainly in small establishments, where lesser benefits are provided because the parties are unable to afford the broader basic protection now contemplated. These establishments, employing a smaller number of employees, are the ones who might incur a substantial increase in costs or an effect on employment. To minimize the burden that will result, a ceiling should be placed on contributions required of both employers and employees. Such an increase in cost for smaller employers can be looked on as equivalent to an increase in the minimum wage. Congress should take this into account in considering increases in the minimum wage.

Where costs exceed the specified ceiling, there should be a sharing of costs through insurance pooling. Preferably this mechanism should be nationally based to overcome the uneven burden created by low-income areas and states. The development of the pooling arrangements and the collection and allocation of funds would be under the general supervision of a National Health Insurance Advisory Board described later in this chapter. One carrier or a consortium of carriers might be chosen to act on behalf of others, as is now occasionally done in some nationwide insurance transactions. In this way, employer and employee contributions could meet the excess cost of some groups and sustain the program for employment-based plans without subsidy from general revenues.*

Latitude should be allowed for rates to reflect the variations in cost for appropriate regional areas. A data base to determine such regions probably already exists; its validity could be refined and modified with experience.

We recommend that the premiums for employment-based plans be financed typically by employer and employee contributions. No employer

---

*See Memorandum by MR. DANIEL F. EVANS, page 94.

or employee should be required to contribute more than a stipulated maximum proportion of the basic insurance premiums. However, there should be an exception to this principle in those cases where an employer has elected to bear more than his required share of the cost.* In order to limit the respective contributions both of employers and employees to the specified levels, an insurance pooling mechanism should be established.

Direct payments for care should be fixed, known, and predictable amounts that in total should not exceed a stipulated percentage of cost of treatment nor in the aggregate of family income.

2. *Insurance for the aged and disabled.* Medicare would continue to cover aged persons insured under the social-security and railroad-retirement acts, as well as persons eligible for disability benefits under both acts who have been brought into Medicare. This has added some 1.7 million people to the present Medicare coverage of more than 20 million. Medicare is the largest single health-insurance plan and one of the best run in the nation. Although the plan is not without problems, the system serves its present and potential beneficiaries well, and its difficulties are susceptible of correction.

Under consideration is the possible consolidation of the present two parts of Medicare into a more consistent and universal program. Likewise, experimentation is going forward with improved methods of reimbursement for care, stressing incentives for economical operations. Other improvements might be suggested, such as coverage of periodic health examinations and immunizations to emphasize prevention, early detection of disease, and health maintenance, as we propose in other categories. The insurance program, rather than the beneficiaries, might bear more of the burden of increasing hospital costs now largely passed on to the insured in the form of increasing deductibles.[3]

We believe that, with certain modifications such as this, Medicare should continue to be financed as at present out of the contributions of employers, employees, beneficiaries, general revenues, and copayments.

3. *Insurance for all other people.* This category not only would provide coverage for all people not otherwise insured, but also would

---

3/The Part A deductibles have increased from an original $40 to a scheduled $72 on January 1, 1973. A simpler and probably more satisfactory provision might be to require a uniform $5 daily copayment during hospitalization rather than the present increasing deductibles and the $10 copayments from the 60th to 90th days of hospitalization.

*See Memorandum by MR. JOHN D. HARPER, page 92.

have the vitally important function of providing continuity and preventing any lapse in basic coverage.

Community trusteeships would be developed to perform for this group the equivalent function to that performed by employers and employees in employment-based plans. The trustees would be responsible for seeing to it that every person who is entitled is insured and receives his benefits. These community organizations would act as advocates for their beneficiaries, procuring better health care for them and responding to community needs. They would reach out to provide services by establishing neighborhood facilities or by offering such transportation for the indigent as is required. These agencies would be federally sponsored and supervised. Where qualified, agencies of state and local governments might be delegated to act as community trusteeships.

The basic benefits under the third category would be the same as those proposed for the employment-based plans. The financing, however, would be related to income, family size, and employment status. The contributions of the poor would be provided by the federal government out of general revenues. Copayments would not be required of the poor and would be reduced for the near-poor. The self-employed could either certify that they had acquired protection under a plan meeting the basic benefit specifications, or enroll in an approved plan by contributing the combined employer-employee premiums.

The insurance coverage under community trusteeships would be financed by general-revenue support for the poor and near-poor and, where appropriate, through a sliding scale of contributions according to such variables as income and family size. Persons whose income is below national poverty standards, whether or not they are receiving welfare assistance, should be relieved of both premiums and copayments; these should be financed by the federal government.

The funds to be made available by the federal government and from the contributions required should reflect regional costs of basic benefits, administration, and reserves. Savings in the cost of basic benefits may be used to expand protection and to provide incentive and support for improved benefits.

Eventually, Medicaid would be replaced almost entirely by the proposed program both through the expansion of employment-based coverage and benefit standards and by the operations of the community trusteeships. A need would still remain for residual assistance on a reduced basis, as some persons covered by the three categories of insurance would exhaust their benefits. Some would require care not covered by the insurance. These might be eligible under a reconstituted aid program, federally financed. Medicaid might also be used for such other purposes as providing high-priority services for the poor before these services can be included in the insurance benefits.

Administration of the Program

The administration of the contemplated national insurance program raises formidable questions of supervision, of impact on delivery of care, and of public responsibility. Public policy clearly requires that the national health-insurance statute set the overall policies and criteria determining whether a plan conforms to its standards and whether a carrier or provider of care is qualified to participate. The Secretary of Health, Education, and Welfare would be responsible for the general direction of the program. Its regulation would be the combined responsibility of the federal and state governments, planning agencies, and regional organizations that are suggested. The states would conduct ongoing review of rates and would protect beneficiaries against the hazards of carrier or plan insolvency.

To guide and operate the program, we propose an administrative structure consisting of certain new and necessary components along with the strengthening and expansion of present functioning mechanisms.

1. A National Health Insurance Advisory Board should be established to guide national policy regarding health insurance.

In order to assure an overall health-insurance policy and to achieve coordination among the component programs, we recommend the creation of a National Health Insurance Advisory Board, appointed by the President and serving in an advisory role to the Secretary of Health, Education, and Welfare. Its membership would comprise public members, as well as health practitioners, administrators, or educators.* The board would be responsible for reviewing the overall regulations directing the insurance program; the timeliness and appropriateness of scheduled phasing of benefits; and the guidelines for evaluating existing employment-based benefit programs and proposed changes in them for compliance. The board's report on the status of the program to the Secretary would be made available to Congress and the nation.

---

*See Memorandum by MR. DANIEL F. EVANS, page 92.

The board would receive reports on the operations of all plans within a uniform record-keeping system and be responsible for the integration of information. It would develop guidelines for relating health insurance to manpower, facilities, funding, and organization of care. It would strive for consistency, coordination, and cooperation among the various component parts of the insurance program. It would evaluate benefit standards and levels, achievement problems, and all other aspects of the program. It would make recommendations regarding phased progression of the program and guide the major policy direction.

Another major function of the board would be to set guidelines for reviewing the features and operations of benefit plans. It would review generally the operations of pooling arrangements to aid plans where costs exceed the specified level.

2. The role of Medicare should be continued and expanded. The present Medicare structure would be utilized as fully as possible in developing the new national health-insurance program.

We believe that the Medicare program should continue to be administered as at present. The administrators of Medicare would assume added responsibility for overseeing the community trusteeships nationally and receive and disburse funds through the existing regional structure for the benefits provided through community trusteeships.

Many areas of cooperation should be cultivated between the employment-based plans, Medicare, and the community trusteeships. For example, the certification of providers such as hospitals, extended care facilities, and laboratories could be extended and uniformly applied so that there would be essentially uniform conditions of participation for all providers of service. Innovative features developed in one sector, such as successful new benefits and methods of reimbursement, might be applied by the others. The National Health Insurance Advisory Board would be available to evaluate such features and act as a clearinghouse for disseminating information on the wider application of such provisions.

Controlling Costs

Medical-care inflation arises mainly from three sources—excess demand relative to limited resources, insensitivity of patients and physicians to fees when a third party is paying the bill, and the cost-plus method of reimbursing hospitals and other providers.* Most health-insurance plans have not yet evolved a truly satisfactory method of reimbursement that can be uniformly prescribed for a national program. However, various methods and experiments are being attempted, the most promising in our view being capitation payments, which we have discussed. We endorse efforts by carriers to assume greater responsibility for the quality and the cost of care through more effective means of surveillance.

It is now widely recognized that the prevailing methods of reimbursing providers under health insurance reduce incentives to contain costs. There are many proposals for new methods of reimbursement. The Administration proposes "prospective reimbursement" under which rates would be set for the coming year. If the institution's costs are lower, it could retain the savings; if costs exceed the prospective rate, the institution risks loss. Budget negotiation is favored by others on the grounds that this would allow the institution to exercise initiative. If goals are set there is a clear idea of what must be accomplished; the buyer can then be more concerned about the quality and quantity of care.

It is now increasingly accepted that the provider of health services should not be able to escape the consequence of bad judgment in underestimating the budget and still recover his additional expenditures. A threshold of quality and quantity should be established and monitoring procedures installed to assure that the provider is also at risk—not only the purchaser and patient.

A comprehensive approach to "controlled charges" has been set forth by Governor Rockefeller's Steering Committee on Social Problems.[4] This would provide for a standard system of accounting and cost finding, budgeting, and review and monitoring, the last to include procedures for challenging and correcting inefficient and unjustified charges. We endorse this general approach and favor its widespread application.

Without the effective exercise of trusteeship, no insurance plan can hope to function well. Much can be accomplished where employers, carriers, or others concerned are willing to assume trusteeship for health plans. One employer reports installing in a hospital a complete cost-centered management and cost-accounting system where one had not existed previously. At a cost of $5,000 a quarter of a million dollars was saved in one institution alone. In another case, the same employer spent about $18,000 of manpower in clerical procedural development at a saving of $128,000—an investment regarded as worthwhile by the company.

4/New York State. Governor's Steering Committee on Social Problems, *Report on Health and Hospital Services and Costs* (1971).
*See Memorandum by MR. D. C. SEARLE, page 90.

Because market forces work imperfectly to supply health care at reasonable costs, we believe that it would be advisable during the inauguration of a national health-insurance program to keep governmental controls over some or all health-care fees, charges, and wages to avoid runaway costs during the transitional period.

This recommendation is consistent with policies previously set forth by this Committee.[5] It is also the course recommended by the Administration for Phase 3 of wage-price controls.

Although market influences generally are preferable to controls, these have been shown to work inadequately in the health industry which is inherently monopolistic. The extension of insurance coverage, benefits, and financing will further modify market influences. Controls therefore undoubtedly will be needed until major structural changes have been accomplished and the national health-care program has been stabilized and is functioning satisfactorily.

5/*High Employment Without Inflation: A Positive Program for Economic Stabilization* (New York: Committee for Economic Development, July 1972), pp. 38-40.

Chapter Six

Coordinated Planning and Use of Resources

Many conflicts and difficulties have inhibited the effective planning of resource development and utilization in the health-care field. In general, the obstacles to planning in health care are similar to those that impede planning in other sectors of American society, arising from the complexities and overlapping functions inherent in the federal-state-local system of government. And in the medical field particularly there are sensitive relationships between the private and public sectors.

Obstacles to planning health functions and facilities have included not only struggles over the sovereignty of separate institutions, but also shortages of planners, know-how, and funds for planning. Much planning is remote from actual conditions in the field. Planning agencies have little control over the funds that are available. Their modest approval powers can often be thwarted, and the scope of their authority is often inherently limited by being too closely tied to the conventional delivery system. Even where planning bodies have aspired to take positive leadership, their actions have been essentially negative because of the need to resist overexpansion of facilities and equipment. Particularly at the state level, these bodies have tended to be captives of the providing groups, and this will continue to pose problems, consumer participation notwithstanding.

Planning executives should function not only by gathering the necessary data and resisting needless expansion but also by developing programs addressed to the health needs of the planning jurisdiction, i.e., "action planning" as advocated by the National Commission on Community Health Services. Responsibility for planning specific programs must be placed on the different levels consistent with the breadth of responsibility of the planning agencies. Fortunately, even though the nation's efforts at health planning have been halting, the basis has been created for developing effective planning mechanisms—particularly at the vitally important regional level.

Among the landmarks in the development of planning, a few are particularly noteworthy. The Hill-Burton Hospital Survey and Construction Act in 1946 was the nation's first major venture into facilities planning and is one of the most significant pieces of national health legislation. It initiated state plans for health facilities. In the years since, planning agencies have begun to look at health facilities in terms of public need, necessary expansion to meet long-range demand, and avoidance of duplication of expensive equipment. The passage in New York of the Metcalf-McCloskey Act in 1964 and the Folsom Act the following year represented major efforts to provide a statutory base for such planning. Increasingly, proposals are made for other states to enact legislation providing for planning bodies that in the words of the Advisory Committee on Hospital Effectiveness have "the power to prohibit construction or expansion of health facilities where such construction or expansion conflicted with the development of an efficient system of health-care delivery for the community."[1]

The federal Partnership for Health legislation in 1966 and 1967, authorizing comprehensive health planning on a state- and area-wide basis, marked a significant advance. These acts consolidated categorical programs allowing grants to be used for those health purposes deemed most important in meeting specialized or regional needs. They authorized the creation of regional comprehensive health-planning agencies, known as "B" agencies, funded by the federal government with matching local

---

1/U.S. Department of Health, Education, and Welfare, *Report to the President on Medical Care Prices* (1967), p. 6.

grants both public and private. The comprehensive health-planning programs have helped bring about a view of regional planning based on the useful concept of what is often now called the health-services trade area, which can be a Standard Metropolitan Statistical Area (SMSA) or an even larger area.

Some comprehensive health-planning agencies have been able to perform effectively despite limitations in authority and purview. They have only review-and-comment jurisdiction over state and local planning agencies; and they lack the funding, administrative capability, and the mandate to implement their own planning—more often than not a fatal weakness in any planning structure. What is significant is the direction in which these agencies are headed and the basis they provide for truly effective planning on a regional basis.

Regional Health Service Agencies

The onset of a national health-care program creates a need for a more effective planning mechanism at the regional level than now exists. There is precedent for the wide-ranging powers that we suggest should be lodged in such a regional agency. Congressional legislation encouraging and funding planning on a regional basis includes housing, highways, mass transit, airports, and other facilities and resources of vital importance to society. The mission of the agency we envisage would be to bring together both the financing and delivery functions of health care, using the new financial resources developed though a national health-insurance program to plan and foster improvements in the delivery system.

We recommend that wherever they exist the presently authorized comprehensive health-planning organizations ("B" agencies) be converted by order of the Secretary of Health, Education, and Welfare into Regional Health Service Agencies, that such agencies be established for all health service regions which lack them, and that their governing boards be appointed initially by the Secretary.* Their powers should be augmented to include the planning of facilities and resources, the review of those presently existing, and development of priorities for improvement. They should have authority to delegate tasks to other planning agencies handling these functions and to assume planning functions of other agencies that are performing inadequately. They should be empowered to encourage, support, and authorize organizations to develop comprehensive

---

*See Memorandum by MR. ROBERT T. FOOTE, page 93.

health-maintenance programs according to approved guidelines and standards for better service and lower cost. They should be responsible for supervising the quality of service and might be delegated as needed to administer price controls over health services in their areas. They also might organize and manage regional information and health-education networks and administer the Public Health Service programs in their areas.

The Regional Health Service Agency would determine the need for new delivery systems or components within the context of the total availability of facilities and services in the region. Where a project or facility did not have its approval, an RHSA could withhold federal moneys in the form either of federal grants and other aid for construction and similar purposes or of funds generated under the national health-insurance system. Contracts between health-maintenance organizations and government for the care of people insured under community trustee-ships would have to be approved by the RHSA on behalf of Medicare. This would also serve to bring pricing arrangements under control.

A major function of the RHSA would be to provide technical assistance for developing health-maintenance organizations in the region, including such matters as legal services, marketing, determination of feasibility, and arrangements with providers for services. Once the given HMO was functioning, the RHSA would serve as a review mechanism over the delivery system, ascertain whether or not it was living up to the standards and guidelines, and provide ongoing technical aid as needed. For smaller HMOs, the RHSA could help arrange for or even provide itself a continuing fiscal-management function.

The Regional Health Service Agency could be the organizer and manager of an information network for its region, possibly linked with a nationwide network. This would collect, analyze, and disseminate data on morbidity, mortality, utilization of services, rates and fees, and other vital matters. It is possible that such a network could provide the basis for a much needed data bank for patient information. The RHSA could also become the center for regional health-education programs for schools and for consumers broadly. If the nation's level of health is to be improved, it is evident that people generally must have greater knowledge not only of the medical resources available to them but also of the responsibility they have for safeguarding their own health and preventing accidents and illness.

Few metropolitan areas have any instrumentality of local government suited to the creation and management of an RHSA of the kind described, nor do counties and cities offer good prospects for a suitable governmental control mechanism. The power to establish RHSAs should be lodged in the Secretary of Health, Education, and Welfare, who would initially appoint the governing board. Because it is essential that the RHSA not be controlled by those who provide the services, a majority of the governing board should comprise public members.

A National Manpower Program

In examining the question of shortages of medical personnel, especially physicians, we have been impressed by the possibility that the existing supply, with its projected rate of increase, could provide the health care called for in our recommendations. This possibility can be realized only by a drastic relocation of resources and an equally drastic reorganization of the health-care delivery system. Changes of such magnitude cannot be made quickly in a free society. Given the pace of change possible with the adoption of our recommendations, some augmentation of resources will be needed.

There is a great need for a national health-manpower policy to replace the present fragmented and spasmodic training of personnel. To stimulate training without a national plan could continue to produce more specialists of some kinds in a single city than the entire nation may need. Manpower may continue to be misused. As is now increasingly evident, more manpower by itself will not curtail the cost increases unless the delivery system is improved.

Under foreseeable conditions, national health-manpower policy should be designed with the intent of developing the requisite personnel and skills to (1) alleviate certain general shortages, (2) overcome the geographic maldistribution in inner-city and rural areas, (3) provide primary care, and (4) staff the new delivery systems, which will be operated to a greater extent by allied health manpower. The fundamental need is for a large increase in the number of allied health workers and in the actual delegation of responsibilities by physicians to capable and appropriately trained assistants.

Training of physicians. Efforts have been made to increase the number of medical schools and their graduates. In 1972, freshman enrollment in 113 medical schools is expected to exceed 11,600, an increase of 23 per cent over the five years 1968-1972. This compares with an increase of only 7 per cent over a like period prior through 1965. Estimates of entering medical students run as high as 13,630, which would go far to close the gap to the 15,300 new entrants proposed for 1976 by the Carnegie Commission on Higher Education. Federal grants have supported the development of ten new medical and dental schools.

Special efforts are being made to develop primary-care physicians. This includes special training in family medicine for M.D.s, and training of physician assistants. Primary-care physicians, as conceived in the American Medical Association's study *The Graduate Education of Physicians* would care for the whole person. They would be the agent of first contact to provide entry into the health system and serve as primary medical resource and counsellor to an individual or family. The new family-practice residency programs attempt to develop specialty training and to provide status, knowledge, and a working model for M.D.s practicing a high quality of family medicine. As of 1970, more than 1,000 approved residencies existed and 5,000 are projected for the year 1975. Continued governmental support of the family-practice residency programs is vitally important as one means of increasing family physicians.

Physician training should be linked with programs designed to redistribute physicians to areas of need. As one means of meeting the shortage, Congress passed legislation in 1970 establishing a National Health Service Corps. The corps provides health services to areas designated by the Secretary of Health, Education, and Welfare by assigning public-health service professionals to these communities. Some 600 professionals are expected to be placed in about 200 areas of need. Physicians can fulfill a draft obligation by service in the corps. They are carefully matched to the community in the hope that they will elect to reside there following service in the corps. The Carnegie Commission has recommended the additional use of financial incentives, i.e., forgiveness of 25 per cent of the maximum indebtedness and deferment of repayment of loans during the period of service.

We believe that physicians and other health personnel will be responsive to financial and other incentives to locate where they are needed in much the same way as other professionally trained people. Forgiveness of part of the debt incurred in training is but one part of a locational incentive program. Such inducements as those offered by practice in HMOs—e.g., salary differentials, living quarters, and opportunities for leisure—should also be part of the program. We urge that these incentives be applied as necessary, and they can be applied under the financing program that we have suggested.*

---

*See Memorandum by MR. D. C. SEARLE, page 93.

However, it remains doubtful whether the trend toward specialization will be readily reversed or that the family-practice residency program or other programs will produce the volume of primary care needed. The key ultimately lies in more efficient utilization of the physician's skill.

Training of health manpower. Programs now going on throughout the country provide training of new categories of health professionals. Some seek substitutes for physicians, while others are also addressed to new and additional health services.

As noted earlier, the recent efforts to develop HMOs, neighborhood health centers, ambulatory-care units, and other new delivery systems have focused on the growing need for new categories of professionals to provide additional services for the prevention and cure of illness and care of the individual.[2] The transfer of tasks from the physician to an assistant allows for increased efficiency and productivity in the delivery of health services. The MEDEX physician-assistant program, for example, offers short and intensive formal training courses (three months) to experienced and skilled ex-military corpsmen followed by one year of internship with a physician.

Likewise, there are programs for expanding the role of the nurse as physician assistant in highly specialized clinical settings such as coronary care. In general, however, there is insufficient awareness or determination to strengthen the nurses' position in relation to foreseeable demands for nursing care. The National Advisory Commission on Health Manpower has recommended that nursing be made a more attractive profession by such means as appropriate use of nursing skills, increased levels of professional responsibilities, improved salaries, more flexible hours for married women, and better retirement provisions. It is essential that the need for training nurses be given appropriate weight in developing a national manpower policy.

There is also great need to develop training programs for nurses and other assistants in the dental field. Only a scant 6 per cent of people were covered by dental-insurance plans at the end of 1970, but more plans are going into effect and national health insurance may eventually greatly increase the demand for dental care. Increasing the number of graduate dentists will not suffice. The approach to dental manpower has been too largely attuned to present demand, not to the potential require-

---

2/People in low-income areas are being trained in allied health services. This serves a double purpose. It opens new employment and career opportunities and also develops a new kind of health professional who can reach out to all people. This will aid in bringing about a more positive, health-oriented system.

ments if the use of dental services were to become more uniformly distributed. In developing a national health-manpower program, there is need for an examination of all dental-manpower requirements including auxiliary personnel.

Allied health-manpower training programs are growing both in kind and in number, many of them sponsored by the federal government. A number of separate governmental departments and agencies are involved. By far the greatest number of paramedical trainees (62,600 in 1972) are supported by the Department of Labor under the Manpower Development Training Act. Such training is also conducted by the Veterans Administration (8,400), Agency for International Development (6,300), Department of Defense (6,000), and, to a markedly lesser extent, by the Department of Health, Education, and Welfare (1,200), and still other agencies (280). Spreading these efforts across so many agencies in separate programs could result in a failure to coordinate goals and objectives; this could impair the experimental design and the evaluation that are particularly important in such a new field.

We recommend increased support and development of health-manpower training programs following systematic central planning by a national health-manpower program located in the office of the Secretary of Health, Education, and Welfare. This office should have a central clearing function to coordinate the goals, data collection methods, and overall design of individual efforts into a broader base for support and evaluation. It should collaborate with the Department of Labor and other departments and agencies to integrate the efforts of the many separate programs of government.

In addition to coordinating experimental design of training programs, efforts should be made to focus attention on common problem areas such as mobility, certification, and remuneration. Career mobility is affected laterally, horizontally, and geographically by the degree of agreement and acceptance of training and certification. Where possible, individual training programs should be coordinated and brought into association with goals and objectives developed by national professional bodies such as the American Medical Association, American Nurses' Association, Association of Schools of Allied Health Professions, and the American Dental Association. There should be strenuous coordinated effort to prevent the creation of dead-end jobs, overspecialization, and training of nonemployable personnel.

Licensure and other legal problems. At present each state has jurisdiction of licensing and certification of health personnel, with wide variations among the states. The result is a restriction of efficient use and mobility of a new health labor force.

Decisions concerning licensure and certification are often influenced by physicians more aware of professional than of broad institutional needs. Because of custom and restrictive regulations, administrators have insufficient leeway to utilize this work force efficiently. The managers of a health-care organization should be able to assert accepted managerial prerogatives having to do with the composition of the work force, reassignment of tasks, creation or elimination of jobs, and so forth.[3] Truly effective use of allied manpower will also require improved analytical tools to define functions more precisely and determine more accurately the number of people required.

State laws such as the Blue Cross and Blue Shield enabling acts sometimes limit the manner of reimbursement for services carried out by newer kinds of professionals such as physician assistants. For example, if the enabling act limits the reimbursement to services performed by a licensed physician, then services performed by the assistant and billed as such cannot be reimbursed. These charges therefore appear on the physician's bill in accordance with laws that allow him to bill only for such services carried out under his direct supervision. However, such a procedure may inflate the fees for these services; it implies billing for an assistant's services at the going physician fee when the use of physician assistants might justify a lower rate than that charged for the physician's direct service. Medicaid regulations offer another kind of restriction; these require that direct supervision must take place in the same office, thus limiting efficient utilization of newly trained personnel.

We recommend the establishment of national guidelines for licensure and certification of health personnel to increase the job mobility and potential use of the health labor force. We expect that most state standards already meet or could easily match the national guidelines.

Development Research in Health Services

To develop the appropriate planning, organization, and training needed to improve the nation's health delivery system will require greatly intensified and sustained research and development. Total expenditure on all medical and health-care research is about $2 billion annually—

3/Anthony Robbins, "Allied Health Manpower—Solution or Problem?" *New England Journal of Medicine*, Vol. 286, No. 17 (April 27, 1972), pp. 918-923.

somewhat less than 3 per cent of the total national expenditure on health. This is devoted overwhelmingly to *basic* research for improved cures for illness and the treatment and prevention of disease. Only some $300 million—four-tenths of one per cent of total expenditures—was devoted to health *services* research. The niggardly expenditures for the development component of R & D in health care is a clear indicator of neglect in this vital aspect of our third largest industry. It quantifies one of the reasons for the underdevelopment of the delivery system.

Our 1968 policy statement, *Innovation in Education: New Directions for the American School,* noted that of industry's total research and development funds, about 4 per cent were expended on basic research, while applied research accounted for nearly 19 per cent and development for 77 per cent. We observed that though there is need for more basic research in education, "there is an immediate demand for more extensive developmental work which will evaluate and apply the findings of research and demonstrate their practical worth." This comment about R & D in education applies with equal or perhaps even greater force to health care.

The nation cannot have an effective and efficient health enterprise and continue to allocate negligible sums for research and development. In June 1970, the Task Force on Medicaid and Related Programs, better known as the McNerney task force, suggested that 5 per cent of federal Medicaid and Medicare funds be used for developing and improving health services and resources. It gave priority to the development of such services and concepts as organized primary health care in neighborhoods; home health-care programs and other alternatives to inpatient hospital care; social and other outreach services that are an integral aspect of appropriate utilization of services; and ways to link and relate new and existing health services with each other, aiming toward comprehensive health-care systems.

Similar proposals are made in the Kennedy-Griffiths bill, which would allocate up to 5 per cent of a proposed trust fund to a resources development fund for systematic and greatly stepped-up developmental activities. The funds would be used to "support innovative health programs, particularly in manpower education, training, group practice development, and other means to improve the delivery of health care." It would come into operation during the "tooling up" period with an appropriation of $200 million two years before benefits begin.

In our 1971 policy statement, *Improving Federal Program Performance,* we recommended that "deliberately planned experimental programs be used more often by federal agencies to gather information as a basis for program design, planning, and evaluation." Further, we urged that funds be included in legislation authorizing experimental programs. We believe that in no sector of American life is this more vitally necessary than in health care.

We recommend that increasing public and private funds be made available for experimental and demonstration programs designed to improve the delivery of health care in amounts consistent with tooling up and with the capability of their prudent use. The responsibility for generating principles and standards for the expenditure of these funds should be vested with the Secretary of Health, Education, and Welfare, in such a manner as to maximize their availability to agencies, both private and public, that are dedicated to and actively involved in the delivery of health care.*

---

*See Memorandum by MR. D. C. SEARLE, page 94.

Memoranda
of Comment, Reservation,
or Dissent

Page 11—By D. C. SEARLE:

The revolutionary advances that have been achieved in health care have admittedly left serious deficiencies to be corrected. Indeed, such progress creates new deficiencies by generating new demands faster than resources can be mobilized to fill them. The critical importance of health care obviously requires serious efforts to correct these problems and, therefore, to analyze the complex issues involved.

It is easy enough to list the deficiencies that exist in this area, as in education, transportation, and many other areas in both the private and public sectors. And harsh judgments of our existing system and its performance make it easy to argue for drastic reorganization. But such proposals raise serious questions.

First, are they based on an objective judgment of our health-care system, that fully accounts for the benefits achieved and measures them against realistic standards?

Second, do they reflect a serious effort to identify and analyze the causes of deficiencies as objectively as possible?

Third, do they offer specific measures to provide specified benefits—a definitive program that could be implemented, and whose costs and benefits could be estimated with reasonable confidence?

Fourth, are they backed by convincing, logical explanations of how and why they would better mobilize our resources and technology to deliver the benefits claimed for them?

A careful review of these proposals has convinced me that they fail on all counts, seriously enough to justify my vote of dissent. To substantiate this assessment, I have inserted footnotes citing a few of the many examples of the bias, inconsistency, and vagueness noted throughout the study.

While the CED study calls for experimentation, its emphasis on reorganization serves to limit the opportunity for serious trials of alternative approaches to delivering better health care. Analysis should be augmented by serious experimental trials of the more promising proposals. Our initial steps must be tentative. Pending such efforts to gain the experience needed to weigh the benefits achieved against the costs incurred—rather than those promised— proposals for sweeping and irreversible reforms are premature and inconsistent with a serious concern for improvement of health care. This Committee should not take the position of endorsing such proposals.

Pages 12 and 32—By D. C. SEARLE:

This line of reasoning provides a clear example of the misplaced prejudice against the profit motive, and of the simplistic explanations that result from such doctrinaire views. What the study fails to note is the rather basic (and obvious) fact that these six high-income states contain the largest urban concentrations—where, incidentally, the per capita figures grossly overstate typical income levels and where even the disadvantaged have access to medical care that is not available to the more affluent members of smaller communities. The point to be stressed is that modern medical technology is oriented not to affluence per se, but to urban society. And this is unavoidably so; only large, concentrated populations can support the degree of specialization and the capital-intensive facilities required to deliver the best of modern technology. The problem of delivering adequate care to the more sparsely populated areas is thus seen to be a far different—and far more difficult—one than this study would suggest.

Page 12—By D. C. SEARLE:

A head count of primary-care physicians is most inadequate as a measure of capacity. It reflects neither the dramatic increase in their productivity and effectiveness nor the declining share of total medical care for which they are responsible.

Page 17—By OSCAR A. LUNDIN, with which THEODORE O. YNTEMA has asked to be associated:

There is little question that a full and thorough discussion of our nation's health problems on an objective basis is both needed and timely. While I am in agreement with the broad goal of promoting and assuring a high level of health care for every person in our country, I feel this policy statement does not clearly indicate how the proposed recommendations would fulfill these health-care needs. Basically, we are confronted with a twofold but dissimilar problem: (1) how to provide adequate health care to all citizens who cannot afford to pay and (2) how to improve the delivery of health services at a reasonable cost to all citizens who can afford to pay. The proposals contained in this statement reflect the weakness inherent in proposing a universal solution to these problems.

Page 17—By D. C. SEARLE:

This concern over faulty allocation of resources could refer either to a need for better allocation of the resources existing *within* the health-care system, or to a need to allocate a larger share of our total resources *to* the health-care area. It would not be unreasonable, of course, to argue that there is room for improvement on both counts. The disturbing feature of this study is not its ambiguity on this point, but its apparent inconsistency. The proposals for drastic reorganization are based on the view that the existing resources are relatively ample, and that substantial improvements could be achieved at little or no cost simply by correcting the virtual lack of organization that is said to characterize the exising "nonsystem." Yet the proposals for financing the system cite the need for attracting new resources to substantially expand its capacity.

Page 18—By D. C. SEARLE:

This analysis reflects a general failure to recognize the dramatic advances that have been achieved in health care, and a tendency to confuse the problems that are associated with progress—the costs of delivering a greatly expanded set of benefits and the impossibility of meeting the instant demands created by every advance—with retrogression. By understating the increase in benefits delivered, it overstates the increase in costs. One consequence of this basic confusion, which permeates the analysis, is an exaggerated notion of the improvements that could be achieved at little or no cost, simply by reorganizing the system.

Pages 18 and 56—By WAYNE E. THOMPSON, with which FRANKLIN A. LINDSAY and RUSS M. JOHNSON have asked to be associated:

In developing a national health-care system, we must focus on the deliberate creation of a competitive free-enterprise market for health-care services. We need a true market in health services that will allow the public to exercise a choice among competing modes in health-care delivery, with patient satisfaction and results determining economic survival of provider components. There should be a major role for private capital and management paralleling the rest of the nation's industrial system.

Our health-care industry is the only major industry that has not had to submit to the discipline either of the marketplace or of public regulation. As a result, the industry has inadequate cost-control mechanisms, and the rate of rise in health-care costs has far outstripped that of any other segment of our economy.

Pages 18, 23, and 74—By D. C. SEARLE:

It is difficult to reconcile the proposed emphasis on prepayment with two other concerns that are developed at some length in this study.

First, a strong case is made for protecting the individual against the potentially disastrous costs of serious illness—i.e., for providing true insurance against the less likely but more serious risks. Yet, the proposals switch the emphasis to concentrate instead on prepayment of routine care and reasonably predictable costs.

Second, the study repeatedly stresses certain tendencies of prepayment programs to be self-defeating. These include the indifference to prices paid by third parties, the similar indifference to total costs incurred and resulting tendency to overburden the system, and the incentives created for hospitalizing patients unnecessarily. Yet, having cited them as major causes of inflated costs, the study proposes prepayment programs as the principal solution to the problem of meeting those costs. While the study proposes to deal with this problem by imposing price controls, experience shows that such measures—which inevitably involve a cost-plus approach to pricing—further weaken the incentives to control costs.

Page 19—By DANIEL F. EVANS:

The political process in the past few years has tended to disregard actuarial discipline and the rising expense of payroll taxes. Accordingly, I am skeptical and concerned about the cost impact of these proposals. I am not aware of any research on the effect of benefit standards on various segments of the private sector, nor of inquiry being made of subcommittee members concerning the effect on their own firms.

Page 21—By D. C. SEARLE:

It would seem presumptuous even to venture a guess as to the cost of implementing proposals as broad and general as those presented in this study. However, since this estimate amounts to less than $24 per capita, we must conclude that the study has grossly understated either the performance of our health-care system or the cost of correcting its deficiencies.

Page 21—By OSCAR A. LUNDIN, with which THEODORE O. YNTEMA has asked to be associated:

Although Appendix C attempts to compare the estimated costs of this and other health-care proposals, the statement does not give adequate consideration to the costs of the proposal through each progression of benefit phases. I have serious reservations regarding the probability of recapturing a significant portion of the increased costs by the better utilization of resources and by cost reductions resulting from basic management improvements.

Pages 22 and 64—By CATHERINE B. CLEARY:

In view of the reliance the report places on insurance, it is my judgment that there should be some reference to the urgent need for a complete overhaul of the claims procedure. More specifically this would mean (1) a simpler and faster method of handling claims and (2) some method by which the insured can see for himself whether he has in fact received the benefits to which his insurance entitles him.

Pages 23 and 56—By ROBERT T. FOOTE, with which RUSS M. JOHNSON has asked to be associated:

In addition to reflecting efficient organization and procedure, any method of fees to be paid providers should also provide the traditional increase in monetary inducements for individuals that assures excellence in delivery and encourages highly motivated and qualified people to enter the field. Any control of fees and charges should be extremely limited. As recommended, it could involve the Regional Health Service Agencies so long as such agencies include on their governing boards suitable peer representatives of individuals and organizations providing care, as well as representatives of recipients. Regional differences in fees and charges should also be taken into account.

Pages 23 and 61—By MARVIN BOWER:

Experience shows that serving a socioeconomic and racial cross section of the population at a health maintenance organization is a difficult objective, because many doctors are reluctant to work in such a setup.

Pages 24 and 65—By MARVIN BOWER:

Benefits for aliens will need to be carefully controlled in order to minimize or even avoid abuses.

Pages 24 and 70—By JOHN D. HARPER:

Pages 68-70 describe a "ceiling . . . on contributions required of both employers and employees" and a method of financial relief for small employers by sharing of costs through a "pooling mechanism." The sharing of costs is to be accomplished through insurance carriers, thus eliminating the need for subsidy from general revenues.

From a practical viewpoint, it is unlikely that an employer would elect to bear more than his required share of premium cost. In fact, an employer providing benefits in excess of the standards should not be expected to subsidize in any way the benefits programs of employers merely attempting to meet the required standards. Employers providing benefits in excess of the required standards should be excluded from the pooling mechanism until such time as benefits packages are upgraded, so that the pooling will permit premium reductions for all employers and employees because of the increased number of persons sharing the cost of the risks involved. Until benefits packages are standardized for all employers, the use of general revenues to subsidize the cost of health benefits for small employers would be more equitable than increasing the financial burden of those relatively few large companies with comprehensive medical-benefits programs.

Pages 25 and 72—By DANIEL F. EVANS:

The membership of the proposed National Health Insurance Advisory Board should include representatives of the business community with no direct connection to the health industry.

Pages 26 and 78—By ROBERT T. FOOTE:

I feel strongly that the Secretary of Health, Education, and Welfare should not be empowered to appoint the governing boards of the Regional Health Service Agencies. There are two fundamental reasons for this. At all cost, we should not permit politics and/or bureaucracy at any level to influence the composition of regional boards. Likewise, we should avoid the possibility that innovation and creativity are stifled through homogeneity in the type of individuals composing the boards.

There are several successful comprehensive health-planning organizations now functioning. They should be encouraged to continue and to modify their approach in compliance with regulations coming from the federal government. New regional agencies required in sections of the country not now covered should be created by stimulation at the federal level, but they should be peopled by the action of local community, business, and government leaders.

Pages 32 and 81—By D. C. SEARLE:

The concern expressed here (and repeated elsewhere) over the effects of the profit motive would seem to be misplaced. Pursuit of self-interest doesn't distinguish physicians from other members of society, and the implication that they are more exclusively concerned with financial gain probably reverses the truth for the great majority. It certainly does not follow logically from the high prices that their services command. Nor would it explain the alleged tendency to prefer overcrowded specialties and neglect areas of shortage. In any case, the proposals made herein would offer no solution for any such problem—unless, of course, we count the use of the financial inducements suggested on page 81. And that would involve us in another basic inconsistency. The motivations that are cited here as a cause of bad manpower allocation are cited there as a means of ensuring better allocation!

Page 32—By D. C. SEARLE:

The relative productivity of the various medical specialties cannot be inferred from the number of patients treated. Such figures provide little insight into the amount or value of service rendered, and do not support the judgments of shortage and oversupply that are made in this study.

Page 36—By D. C. SEARLE:

The established practice of paying in proportion to what is received extends into every area of economic activity and is based upon considerations of equity. It is central to the very concept of price—and of equity in pricing—and can hardly be said to be a cause of inequitable charges. Nor can it bear any responsibility for inefficient accounting and billing procedures or other problems attributed to it here.

Page 52—By D. C. SEARLE:

This discussion of the advances that have been achieved in mental health serves to illustrate three strengths of our health-care system that are systematically neglected throughout this study—namely, that it has produced remarkable advances in technology; that organizational changes are dependent upon changes of other sorts; and that the system *has* been responsive to changing needs and capabilities. It is interesting to note the concern expressed here over the difficulty of reconciling the innovations in this area with the "comprehensive health-care system" proposed by this study.

Page 60—By MARVIN BOWER:

Experience of health-maintenance organizations to date shows that it is difficult to get doctors to serve in the ghetto areas. Yet the convenience of the patient requires that HMOs be located geographically in neighborhoods which are predominantly of one socioeconomic level.

Page 69—By DANIEL F. EVANS:

Without more information on cost impact, and with reservations concerning the influence of the political process on overall costs, one reasonably could conclude that no policy statement opposing public subsidy should be made at this time.

Page 86—By D. C. SEARLE:

While the study advocates continuing experimentation, the approaches that it proposes for reorganization would greatly curtail the opportunities for testing alternative approaches. It is not clear, for example, how voluntary participation in HMOs can be reconciled with mandatory participation in standardized employment-based insurance programs. Nor would there be any apparent motivation for committing private funds to new ventures in competition with programs mandated and supported by government.

The study further proposes a vast expansion of governmental "planning," which clearly involves the authority not only to plan and recommend but to impose the designs of the planners to regulate the system. Authoritarian measures of this sort are obviously not conducive to innovation.

Appendix A

Ten Basic Steps in Starting
a Health-Maintenance Organization

There is little understanding of the many preliminary steps that must be taken to start a successful health-maintenance organization. Nor is there general recognition of the interrelationship and complexity of these vitally essential procedures (see Figure 8). A delay in any major component of an HMO can stop its entire development. Dovetailing the recruitment of subscribers and of staff, for example, is particularly difficult to achieve. Thus some plans have members enrolled before they are ready to serve them; others recruit staff before their membership is built up, at considerable penalty in cost and morale.

The following checklist of the steps required to develop a viable health-maintenance organization is based on successful attempts to establish prepaid comprehensive programs.

1. *Feasibility study*

Preparation for an HMO should start with a feasibility study that examines the proposed plan in terms of its objectives, the population profile to be covered, and the manpower and other resources available to the organization. This should yield the data necessary for deciding whether to proceed or not.

2. *Formulation of objectives and goals*

Plans sponsored by a medical school, a medical group, a hospital, an industry, a consumer or labor organization, or a community may each have different objectives; these should be made explicit. A statement of objectives and goals sought is essential in order to establish the criteria for setting priorities, defining the plan and scope of operation, drafting a charter, and determining the form of organization. In addition to such broad objectives, specific short- and long-term goals should be formulated to provide a timetable and standards for measuring accomplishment as the plan proceeds.

3. *Development of a planning, operating, and policy-setting organization*

The development of a suitable corporate and administrative structure is secondary only to the decision to proceed. The first step is the designation of a policy-making body (board of directors) composed of persons having the variety of backgrounds and experience most useful to future development. This body must select and empower the operating executive, which must be responsible to it.

The medical delivery system may be organized as a partnership, corporation, association, or single ownership; there are other possible forms, each with its characteristics and advocates. Various basic operational patterns are likewise possible; for example, the management organization may contract with existing medical groups, establish one or more groups for the plan, or aid in establishing an autonomous medical organization. The expertise needed and the cost of developing suitable management services for an HMO make it advisable to separate the management-fiscal component from the delivery system. The management-fiscal organization engages in recruitment of the clientele or population, community relationships, data handling, facility development, fund raising, and so forth. Each HMO has to decide whether it needs to form a new financing mechanism or whether it can rely on an established carrier (or carriers) to provide for prepayment. With large delivery systems, such delegation of functions may be unnecessary and even detrimental. Because of their scale, smaller systems may not be able to develop an adequate managerial mechanism. In each instance, the advantages and disadvantages of an integrated versus a federated organization should be weighed.

4. *Legal development*

Twenty-two states prohibit or limit the group practice of medicine, and laws in many states prevent doctors from delegating to their assistants certain responsibilities, such as giving injections. These illustrations serve to suggest the nature of the legal problem that can hamper the establishment of viable HMOs. There is a need for a review of all applicable laws at an early stage in the development of a proposed health-maintenance organization; later on, legal work is required in obtaining various approvals and certifications.

5. *Population development*

It is necessary to determine the size and composition of the subscribing population, the extent of fee-for-service treatment of nonenrolled patients, the projected scale of the delivery system during the first years of its operation, and the geographic areas to be covered in the various stages of the plan's development. Provision must be made for the education of consumers and for their participation in policy development. Processing of grievances relating to services, benefits, costs, and so forth should become an integral part of the plan.

6. *Determination of the services and benefits to be provided*

A few general principles may be enunciated in designing benefits for an HMO: (1) All subscribers should have access to an organized program of comprehensive care. (2) The basic benefits should offer optimum protection supportable by the premiums. (3) Each of the benefits must be delivered satisfactorily without undue delay. (4) Benefit development should be a continuing process.

7. *Development of one or more delivery systems*

The mix in each HMO of direct versus contracted services and full-time versus part-time personnel is a function of size, resources, and policy. In coping with considerable problems of acquiring its staff in synchronization with the recruitment of membership, a new HMO could start with an expandable core of general practitioners, internists, and a few other primary physicians with arrangements to refer patients to part-time medical staff; full-time specialists could be added as the population grows. Similarly, arrangements could be made with other physicians on a per-session or fee-for-service basis in specialties less often required by the population. In rural areas, different arrangements will be needed; the hospital may play a larger part, and the network of services may be quite different from those in densely populated areas.

Because there has been considerable difficulty in some HMOs with the treatment of patients by part-time physicians, who in addition to their responsibility to the HMO also serve patients on a fee-for-service basis, it may be preferable to employ full-time physicians. This would remove the problem of physicians favoring their private patients at the expense of the prepaid members. The compensation of physicians is often based on specialty and years of experience and training and may include incentive payments, all geared to attract physicians, to remunerate them well for their services, and to motivate them to support the plan's objectives. Benefits from joining the staff of an HMO can include an office; transportation; retirement benefits; life, sickness, long-term disability, and health insurance; sickness and other leaves; conferences; dues in professional associations; malpractice insurance; and time allowed for research, education, and teaching. These constitute a considerable incentive.

8. *Facility development*

Facilities are required to provide suitable location, quality of environment, and access to all levels of care in an integrated network. The several options open include building, purchasing, remodeling, or contracting for use. Corresponding land and capital requirements need to be determined. These determinations are important for any plan and involve not only detailed assessment of cost but also of plan policy.

Although facility requirements appear to be straightforward and readily determinable, they actually pose many questions. Careful study of the facility requirements of HMOs is needed and thus far has not been made. The Task Force for Health Facilities Research has identified facilities for HMOs as a matter requiring urgent investigation. The hospital seeking to shift to programs using fewer beds for inpatient care requires thoughtful preparation, including cost-benefit analysis *and* experimental demonstration. The emerging primary-care centers, surrogates for home care, also urgently need investigation as a possible basic regrouping of health care.

9. *Financial development*

The funding requirements of an HMO generally fall into three major stages. The first is the initial planning of the program, culminating in contracts and arrangements with providers of care, insurance carriers, and members; these are essential in determining the benefit structure and the capitation required to provide the services, operate the plan, repay loans, and so forth.

The second is the preparation of facilities, acquisition of equipment, and recruitment of staff up to the eve of operations. The third is the initiation of operations up to the time that the plan can expect to break even.

In order to determine the costs and income and to develop financial projections, the following steps—well known in business practice but less often understood and applied in health care—are essential. First, there must be a line budget identifying cost categories, showing the estimated utilization rates and costs (per service and per enrollee) for such items as hospital care, physician and nurse services, contracted health care, and supplies and services. Revenues from capitation payments, over-the-counter fees, fee-for-service practice, drugs, eyeglasses, grants, and so forth must be determined. Second, financial projections should show cash flow, income and expenses, and capital needs. These projections may indicate that the plan is not feasible; it may take too long to break even, or it may require more start-up support than is obtainable. They can also aid in the realistic planning, development, and management of the Health Maintenance Organization.

10. *Program for evaluation and research*

Often omitted and generally deferred are provisions for data collection and systematic development of a built-in program of evaluation. From the start, such a program should assure that the goals of the plan are explicit and adhered to. In the general desire to encourage such undertakings, performance is often ignored. Additionally, because of their competitive role, HMOs offer an excellent opportunity for controlled experimentation with different delivery systems that should be evaluated objectively so that these findings may be used elsewhere.

Appendix B

Illustrative Benefit Standard

The following are suggested benefits that might comprise a basic benefit standard in a national health-insurance program. Also shown is a suggested phasing of these individual benefits in four stages over the early years of the program.

The phasing of the benefits would be timed to the development of the delivery system, not to a predetermined time schedule. As facilities and services are made available, successive enlargements of benefits could be offered without increasing inflationary pressures and with assurance that the increased benefits could be delivered to people as promised.

It should be noted that the aggregate amount of copayments specified herein to be paid by an individual or a family would be limited to an annual dollar amount or per cent of income.

Benefits	Phase I	II	III	IV
1. Physician's care in office, ambulatory center, mental-health center, or health-maintenance organization.				
a. First three visits per family member per year: insured pays $2 per visit.	I			
b. Next three visits per family member per year: insured pays $2 per visit.		II		
c. Balance of visits. (For treatment of mental conditions: insured pays 50 per cent. Other conditions: insured pays $5 per visit.)			III	
2. Diagnostic tests, including X rays, laboratory tests, and electrocardiograms.	I			
3. Surgery, including necessary anesthesia, and radiation therapy.	I			

100.

Benefits	Phase I	II	III	IV
4. Family-planning services and supplies.	I			
5. Periodic health checkup examinations.				
a. Well-baby care including immunizations:				
During first two years after birth, not more than twelve visits.	I			
During next three years, not more than three visits.		II		
b. Persons, ages six through thirty-nine, one such examination every five years.		II		
c. Persons, age forty and over, one such examination every two years.		II		
6. Dental care.				
a. Annual oral examination, including prophylaxis and X rays:				
Children under nineteen.			III	
All others.				IV
b. Amalgam filling, extractions, dentures: insured pays 20 per cent:				
Children under nineteen.			III	
All others.				IV
c. Other dental care except orthodontia: insured pays 50 per cent.		II		
7. Drugs requiring a prescription and such non-legend drugs as are specified by the Secretary of Health, Education, and Welfare (e.g., insulin): insured pays $1 per prescription.			III	
8. Rehabilitation services: insured pays 20 per cent.				
a. Prosthetic appliances.		II		
b. Physical therapy.		II		
c. Speech therapy (ambulatory or institutional).			III	
9. Vision care.				
a. Children under nineteen: no more than one examination and one set of frames and lenses per year.			III	
b. All others: no more than one examination and one set of frames and lenses every three years. Insured pays 50 per cent.			III	

Benefits	Phase I	II	III	IV
10. Semiprivate general or psychiatric hospital care per illness: insured pays $5 per day.				
a. First 30 days.	I			
b. Next 90 days (total of 120 days).		II		
c. Next 180 days (total of 300 days).			III	
11. Skilled nursing-home care for convalescent purposes per illness: insured pays $2.50 per day.				
a. First 60 days.	I			
b. Next 60 days (total of 120 days).		II		
c. Next 60 days (total of 180 days).			III	
12. Home-health services per illness when provided as part of an approved home-care program: insured pay $2.50 per day.				
a. First 90 days.	I			
b. Next 90 days (total of 180 days).		II		
c. Next 90 days (total of 270 days).			III	
13. Physician's services while institutionalized.				
a. When rendered on a day for which a benefit is payable for institutional care: insured pays $2 per visit.	I	II	III	
b. When rendered on a day for which a benefit is not payable for institutional care: insured pays $5 per visit.	I	II	III	
14. Maternity care. Prenatal care, including necessary immunizations, delivery and postnatal care: insured pays 20 per cent.	I			
15. Catastrophic coverage. When medical expenses in a year reach $2,000, insured pays 20 per cent of additional covered expenses. Maximum benefit: $100,000.	I			

Appendix C

Estimated Cost of
CED Recommendations

For many reasons it is difficult to calculate the effect on national health expenditures of the proposals described in this statement. Not the least of these inponderables are the long-run results of various recommendations intended to produce improvements in organizational efficiency and utilization of resources, which in turn should affect costs. For lack of any measures by which to quantify these effects, the estimates here are based on the assumption that current practice and organization of health-care services remain unchanged.

In the absence of any new health-care legislation, it can be estimated on the basis of past trends that national health-care expenditures will rise from $83 billion in fiscal 1972 to $114 billion in 1975. Of this latter sum, $66 billion will be spent in the private sector and $48 billion in the public sector. An increase of $5 billion in national health expenditures could be expected to cover the cost of the additional benefits under our proposed plan if all benefits were in effect in 1975. This increase would bring national expenditures to about $119 billion in that year. But the principal effect would be rearrangement of the contributions made by the several participants in the financing system.

Almost the entire net increase would be in government spending which would rise from an estimated $48 billion to $52 billion. Expenditures by state and local government would be nearly $3 billion less than could be anticipated on the basis of past trends, while the spending of the federal government, which would assume more of the burden for financing the health needs of the disadvantaged, should increase by about $7 billion to reach a level of some $43 billion.

The estimated increase of $1 billion or so in total private health expenditures would have far less impact than the considerable shift within the private sector in the source of the contributions. The net increase of $1 billion is the difference between an increase of $14 billion in private health-insurance premium costs and a decrease of $13 billion in individual direct payments to providers. However, of the $14 billion increase in private health-insurance premiums, about one-quarter would be the employees' share. This suggests that a significantly increased responsibility will fall to employers, employees, and carriers to work for economies in the delivery system.

Our estimates are based on the methodology employed by the Department of Health, Education, and Welfare in costing major national health-insurance proposals now pending in Congress. HEW's comparable estimates for other national health-insurance programs for 1974 indicate

National Health Expenditures by Proposal, Fiscal 1974
(in billions)

Proposal	Total	Private sector				Governmental sector		
		Total	Individual direct payments	Health insurance	Other	Total	State and local	Federal
None	$105.4	$62.3	$32.0	$26.4	$3.9	$43.1	$11.1	$32.0
Byrnes	107.2	62.2	28.3	30.0	3.9	45.0	10.0	35.0
Griffiths-Corman	113.8	15.9	11.2	1.9	2.8	97.9	6.5	91.4
Fulton-Broyhill	109.5	61.9	26.5	31.5	3.9	47.6	9.3	38.3
Burleson	110.2	62.3	21.7	36.7	3.9	47.9	8.6	39.3
Dingell	116.8	13.9	6.9	3.1	3.9	102.9	9.6	93.3
Hall	107.6	59.0	28.5	26.6	3.9	48.6	13.4	35.2
Hogan	107.7	59.0	27.8	27.3	3.9	48.7	13.4	35.3
Fisher	109.1	58.1	27.5	26.7	3.9	51.0	8.7	42.3
Bennett	107.2	62.6	28.3	30.4	3.9	44.6	10.0	34.6
Long	106.5	60.3	30.0	26.4	3.9	46.2	11.1	35.1
Javits	113.0	31.3	19.9	8.2	3.2	81.7	8.1	73.6
Pell-Mondale	114.9	67.3	17.3	46.1	3.9	47.6	10.7	36.9
CED[1]	110.4	63.4	19.3	40.2	3.9	47.0	8.6	38.4

1/Estimates by the Committee for Economic Development.

Source: U.S. Department of Health, Education, and Welfare. *Analysis of Health Insurance Proposals Introduced in the 92nd Congress* (1971).

that the increased national health expenditure anticipated from our proposals fall into a mid-range of estimated increases. Distribution effects between and within sectors could vary widely, of course, as is seen in the table on the opposite page. Neither these estimates nor ours take into account the effects of phasing benefits over a period of years.

Honorary Trustees

Trustees on Leave for Government Service

CED Professional and Administrative Staff

PUBLICATION ORDER FORM

To order CED publications please indicate number in column entitled "# Copies Desired." Then mail this order form and check for total amount in envelope to Distribution Division, CED, 477 Madison Ave., New York 10022.

ORDER NUMBER   STATEMENTS ON NATIONAL POLICY (paperbound)   # COPIES DESIRED

49P . . BUILDING A NATIONAL HEALTH-CARE SYSTEM $1.75 _____

Sets forth a plan for the organization, management, and financing of a national health care system which would improve the delivery of health care services while extending insurance coverage to all Americans. Includes an extensive review of the current health care system.

48P . . A NEW TRADE POLICY TOWARD COMMUNIST COUNTRIES $1.50 _____

CED and its counterparts in Europe and Japan propose the creation of a new global economic organization to develop rules governing trade and commercial relations between East and West. In an individual statement, CED recommends a continued easing of U.S. trade and credit restrictions against communist countries, bringing them in line with U.S. policies toward other industrialized nations.

47P . . HIGH EMPLOYMENT WITHOUT INFLATION: A POSITIVE PROGRAM FOR ECONOMIC STABILIZATION $1.50 _____

Recommends a continued governmnetal role in wage-price policies, calls for basic structural changes in the economy, and urges an incentive system of decontrol. Emphasizes that fiscal and monetary policies must remain the key element of the nation's economic efforts.

46P . . REDUCING CRIME AND ASSURING JUSTICE $1.50 _____

An integrated examination of needed reforms in the entire system of criminal justice, including courts, prosecution, police, and corrections.

45P . . MILITARY MANPOWER AND NATIONAL SECURITY $1.00 _____

Focuses on several critical issues relating to military manpower. Recommends an annual review by Congress of the sources and uses of military personnel. This proposal is designed to increase the accountability of the Executive Branch to the public while preserving needed Presidential flexibility in dealing with emergencies.

44P . . THE UNITED STATES AND THE EUROPEAN COMMUNITY $1.50 _____

Deals with the development of the Common Market into an enlarged European Economic Community and its potential effects on Western European trade, investment, and monetary relations with the U.S. and other free-world nations. Recommends immediate steps to halt deterioration in the world trading system.

43P . . IMPROVING FEDERAL PROGRAM PERFORMANCE $1.50 _____

Focuses attention on three major areas of concern about federal programs: (1) the choice of policy goals and program objectives, (2) the selection of programs that will achieve those objectives, and (3) the execution of the programs and the evaluation of their performance.

42P . . SOCIAL RESPONSIBILITIES OF BUSINESS CORPORATIONS $1.50 _____

Develops a rationale for corporate involvement in solving such pressing social problems as urban blight, poverty, and pollution. Examines the need for the corporation to make its social responsibilities an integral part of its business objectives. Points out at the same time the proper limitations on such activities.

41P . . EDUCATION FOR THE URBAN DISADVANTAGED: From Preschool to Employment $1.50 _____

A comprehensive review of the current state of education for disadvantaged minorities; sets forth philosophical and operational principles which are imperative if the mission of the urban schools is to be accomplished successfully.

40P . . FURTHER WEAPONS AGAINST INFLATION $1.50 _____

Examines the problem of reconciling high employment and price stability. Maintains that measures to supplement general fiscal and monetary policies will be needed— including the use of voluntary wage-price (or "incomes") policies, as well as measures to change the structural and institutional environment in which demand policy operates.

39P . . MAKING CONGRESS MORE EFFECTIVE $1.00 _____

Points out the structural and procedural handicaps limiting the ability of Congress to respond to the nation's needs. Proposes a far-reaching Congressional reform program.

38P . . DEVELOPMENT ASSISTANCE TO SOUTHEAST ASIA $1.50 _____

Deals with the importance of external resources—financial, managerial, and technological, including public and private—to the development of Southeast Asia.

37P . . TRAINING AND JOBS FOR THE URBAN POOR $1.25 _____

Explores ways of abating poverty that arises from low wages and chronic unemployment or underemployment. Evaluates current manpower training and employment efforts by government and business.

36P . . IMPROVING THE PUBLIC WELFARE SYSTEM $1.50 _____

Analyzes the national problem of poverty and the role played by the present welfare system. The statement recommends major changes in both the rationale and the administration of the public assistance program, with a view to establishing need as the sole criterion for coverage.

35P . . RESHAPING GOVERNMENT IN METROPOLITAN AREAS $1.00 _____

Recommends a two-level system of government for metropolitan areas: an area-wide level and a local level comprised of "community districts."

SEE OTHER SIDE→

34P . . ASSISTING DEVELOPMENT IN LOW-INCOME COUNTRIES $1.25   _____
        Offers a sound rationale for public support of the U.S. economic assistance program
        and recommends a far-ranging set of priorities for U.S. Government policy.

33P . . NONTARIFF DISTORTIONS OF TRADE $1.00   _____
        Examines the complex problem of dealing with nontariff distortions of trade arising
        from governmental measures that create special barriers to imports and incentives
        to exports.

32P . . FISCAL AND MONETARY POLICIES FOR STEADY ECONOMIC GROWTH $1.00   _____
        Reexamines the role of fiscal and monetary policies in achieving the basic economic
        objectives of high employment, price stability, economic growth, and equilibrium
        in the nation's international payments.

31P . . FINANCING A BETTER ELECTION SYSTEM $1.00   _____
        Urges comprehensive modernization of election and campaign procedures at
        national, state, and local levels. Proposes ways to reduce costs and spread them
        more widely through tax credits.

30P . . INNOVATION IN EDUCATION $1.00   _____
        Examines the problems of the American schools, reviews educational goals and
        opportunities (including technological resources), and explores relative costs and
        benefits. Sets forth comprehensive recommendations for change.

28P . . MODERNIZING STATE GOVERNMENT $1.00   _____
        Recommends sweeping renovation of state governments and their constitutions. Pro-
        poses granting legislatures broad powers to deal with problems of a rapidly-changing
        era; strengthening executive capability through modern management methods; im-
        proving the administration of justice; and furthering intergovernmental relations.

27P . . TRADE POLICY TOWARD LOW-INCOME COUNTRIES $1.50   _____

24P . . HOW LOW INCOME COUNTRIES CAN ADVANCE THEIR OWN GROWTH $1.50   _____

23P . . MODERNIZING LOCAL GOVERNMENT $1.00   _____

22P . . A BETTER BALANCE IN FEDERAL TAXES ON BUSINESS   75¢   _____

21P . . BUDGETING FOR NATIONAL OBJECTIVES $1.00   _____

15P . . EDUCATING TOMORROW'S MANAGERS $1.00   _____

14P . . IMPROVING EXECUTIVE MANAGEMENT IN THE FEDERAL GOVERNMENT $1.50   _____

9P . . ECONOMIC LITERACY FOR AMERICANS   75¢   _____

1P . . ECONOMIC GROWTH IN THE UNITED STATES $1.00   _____

Quantity discounts: 10-24 copies—10%, 25-49 copies—15%, 50-99 copies—20%, 100-249 copies—30%

NOTE TO EDUCATORS: Instructors in colleges and universities may obtain
up to 5 free copies of those CED Statements on National Policy which they in-
tend to use in courses they are teaching. Please mention the course name when
ordering. For more than 5 copies, an educational discount of 20% will apply.
Course..

☐ I am enclosing $.............................. for the copies ordered above.

☐ Please bill me. *(Payment must accompany orders under $10.00)*

DO YOU WANT ALL CED PUBLICATIONS WHEN ISSUED?

☐ I would like to obtain all CED publications as soon as they are issued. Please send
me information about the CED Reader Forum subscription plan.

☐ Please send me newest list of publications.

Name..

Organization..

Address...

City.. State.............................. Zip..............................

    ☐ **Businessman**   ☐ **Educator**   ☐ **Professional**

TEAR OUT ON DOTTED LINE AND MAIL IN ENVELOPE TO CED